Speed Reading: Accelerate Your Learning and Comprehension

Techniques and Strategies to Read Faster and Retain More

David Cooper

Table of Contents

INTRODUCTION

The book "Speed Reading: Accelerate Your Learning and Comprehension: Techniques and Strategies to Read Faster and Retain More" is a comprehensive guide designed to revolutionize your reading and information absorption. In today's fast-paced world, the ability to quickly grasp and understand large volumes of material is more valuable than ever. This book delves into the science of speed reading, offering readers a blend of proven methods and innovative approaches to enhance their reading speed without sacrificing comprehension.

This book provides the tools you require, regardless of whether you are a student who wants to enhance the efficiency of your study, a professional who wants to stay ahead in a competitive sector, or a lifelong learner who is eager to extend your knowledge base. The course covers fundamental ideas such as minimizing subvocalization and increasing peripheral vision, and it also teaches more sophisticated techniques such as meta-guiding and the utilization of digital tools. The book also covers frequent challenges and misconceptions about fast reading and offers answers and advice that may be put into practice to overcome these challenges and misconceptions.

The book "Speed Reading: Accelerate Your Learning and Comprehension" equips readers to apply these strategies in various settings, including academic texts, professional documents, and leisure reading. This is accomplished through a series of interactive exercises and examples from the real world. Not only will you learn to read more quickly with the help of this book, but you will also be able to remember and comprehend more of what you read. This is because the guide emphasizes sustainable practices and continual improvement. Become familiar with this vital resource, and you will be able to unleash the full potential of your reading talents, eliminating the problem of information overload permanently.

CHAPTER I

Understanding Speed Reading

Definition and Importance of Speed Reading

A collection of methods called "speed reading" is intended to help people read and understand text more quickly. Fundamentally, speed reading is teaching the eyes and brain to process longer passages of text more quickly, which shortens the amount of time needed to read and comprehend written content. In our information-rich environment, where assimilating and processing large volumes of information fast can lead to major advantages in both personal and professional contexts, this skill is very valuable.

Although the idea of speed reading has been around for a while, Evelyn Wood is frequently given credit for popularizing the practice in the middle of the 20th century. Wood's strategies centered on reducing subvocalization, or the inner monologue that usually occurs when reading, and promoting the reader's ability to quickly scan several words or even full lines of text. Although her methods established the groundwork for contemporary speed reading, developments in cognitive science and educational psychology have further enhanced these strategies, increasing their efficacy and accessibility for a wider range of users.

The enormous amount of information that people must take in every day is one of the main reasons rapid reading is crucial. Employees in professional environments are frequently deluged with reports, emails, and other papers that require a cursory but in-depth perusal. Students also have to traverse large textbooks, research papers, and other course resources. Faster reading speed and memory retention can result in increased output, greater performance, and more effective use of time.

Additionally, beneficial to academics and personal growth is speed reading. People can study more in less time by speeding up the reading process, which enables them to learn new information and delve into a greater variety of subjects. For lifelong learners who are always looking to learn more and keep up with the newest advancements in their areas of interest, this can be especially helpful.

Some fundamental ideas are combined in the science of fast reading to increase reading efficiency. The decrease of subvocalization is one such idea. The tendency for us to "hear" the words as we read might cause reading to go very slowly. We can read more quickly if we train ourselves to limit this internal dialogue. Reducing subvocalization and maintaining smooth eye movement over the text can be accomplished by employing techniques like utilizing a finger or pointer to guide the gaze.

The development of peripheral vision is another crucial idea. While most readers concentrate on one word at a time, we can see several words at once, thanks to our peripheral vision. Readers can process information more quickly by using tactics that encourage their eyes to take in greater portions of text. Instead of pausing at each word on the page, this method teaches the eyes to move fluidly and sweepingly across the page.

Retention and comprehension are two other essential elements of efficient speed reading. Contrary to popular belief, reading quickly does not imply losing comprehension. In actuality, a lot of speed-reading strategies aim to improve comprehension by promoting active reading. Asking questions, interacting with the text, and drawing connections to previously learned material are all part of active reading. A more in-depth comprehension of the subject matter and improved retention are possible outcomes of this increased engagement with the information.

Additionally, rapid reading is adaptable to a variety of reading materials. For instance, readers may employ a combination of scanning and skimming strategies to swiftly locate the most important details and concepts in lengthy academic publications. While scanning is seeking specific information or keywords, skimming entails swiftly skimming the text to acquire an overall idea of its content. When working with enormous amounts of data or attempting to locate specific information inside a document, these strategies can be quite helpful.

Apart from its pragmatic uses, rapid reading has the potential to enhance cognitive growth. Frequent practice of speed reading can enhance mental agility, focus, and concentration, which can lead to an improvement in total brain function. Rapidly digesting and comprehending complicated information can enhance cognitive flexibility and activate brain pathways, both of which are advantageous in many facets of life.

Speed reading has restrictions and isn't appropriate for all kinds of reading despite its many advantages. For example, reading materials that call for in-depth critical thought, like difficult philosophical texts or literary works, might not be well suited to speed reading methods. In certain situations, reading more slowly and deliberately might be required to properly understand the subtleties and depth of the material.

Additionally, it takes patience, effort, and commitment to become a proficient speed reader. It is not a talent that is quickly picked up. To increase reading comprehension and speed, people need to put in the work to learn new strategies, practice them frequently, and master them. But the long-term advantages of mastering rapid reading can easily offset the time and effort required upfront.

The ability to increase productivity is one of speed reading's biggest benefits. Employees who are fast readers and information processors in the workplace are frequently more productive and successful in their positions. They possess the ability to manage their workload effectively, reply to emails and reports in a timely manner, and make well-informed decisions by fully comprehending pertinent data. Better career progression chances, higher job satisfaction, and improved job performance can result from this.

Reading quickly can be a game-changer for students. Gaining the capacity to read and understand textbooks, research articles, and other academic materials rapidly can improve grades and make learning more pleasurable. More content may be covered in less time, enabling students to take part in class discussions more actively, finish assignments more quickly, and study for tests more skillfully. Additionally, speed reading can lessen the tension and worry that comes with keeping up with a heavy reading load, improving and enriching the educational process in general.

Speed reading can help people become more knowledgeable and open-minded in their daily lives. People who speed read are able to take in more information in less time, whether they are reading novels, self-help books, or the most recent headlines. This can enable people to study a greater range of subjects and concepts, which can result in a more satisfying and intellectually challenging life.

Utilizing the appropriate resources and methods is crucial to maximizing the advantages of speed reading. There are numerous programs and software available for fast reading that can assist people in honing their abilities. These tools can be quite helpful for people who want to increase their reading efficiency because they frequently provide features like progress tracking, highlighting, and customizable reading speeds. E-readers and other digital reading devices can also be helpful because they frequently have built-in features that facilitate rapid reading and make navigation and annotation simple.

Setting up a comfortable reading space is also essential for efficient speed reading. Focus and concentration can be greatly improved by having a location free from distractions, appropriate lighting, and a comfortable seating position. The development of speed-reading abilities can also be facilitated by establishing clear reading objectives and sticking to a regular reading schedule.

Lastly, it's critical to remember that there is no one-size- fits-all approach to fast reading. It could take some experimenting to identify the most effective methods and strategies, as various people may find different tactics and ways to be more successful. Being an effective speed reader can have significant and long-lasting advantages; therefore, the key is to be persistent and patient.

In conclusion, the ability to read quickly is a strong characteristic that has many applications in both personal and professional settings. People can manage information overload, advance their learning and personal growth, and enhance their productivity and cognitive function by developing their reading speed and efficiency. Although speed reading might not be appropriate for every kind of reading material, it is still a useful skill to learn because of the time savings, enhanced comprehension, and information it provides. Anyone can master fast reading and realize the full benefits of this game-changing skill with commitment and practice.

The Science Behind Speed Reading

There is an intriguing interaction between psychological and physiological processes that support speed reading, the skill of quickly absorbing and understanding written material. The scientific basis for speed reading is the discovery of ways to enhance the way the human brain processes visual information. The goal of speed reading is to improve reading speed and comprehension by applying concepts from neuroscience, cognitive psychology, and studies of eye movement. In this section, we will look at the science behind rapid reading, which includes topics like the brain-eye connection, the function of eye movements, the shortcomings of conventional reading strategies, and solutions to increase reading efficiency.

The human visual system is incredibly good at digesting visual information; this is the foundation of speed reading. Our eyes perform a sequence of quick movements called saccades when we read. To scan text, we use saccades, which are rapid, conjoined movements of the eyes in the same direction. The brain processes the visual information gathered during the brief pauses known as fixations that occur between these saccades. It could take a lot of time to read using traditional methods because they require several brief fixes on individual words. Methods for speed reading lessen the frequency and length of these fixations so that the reader can absorb more material in a shorter amount of time.

Speed reading aims to reduce subvocalization, or the internal speaking that happens when we read, which is another important part of conventional reading. Reading more slowly may be the result of subvocalization, in which we mentally pronounce words as we read. Subvocalization aids understanding, but it restricts reading speed to that of internal speech, which is usually about 200-300 words per minute. One goal of speed-reading techniques is to make it easier for readers to interpret material visually instead of aurally by reducing or eliminating subvocalization. Doing so has the ability to boost reading speeds to 400–700 words per minute or even higher.

The practice of honing one's peripheral vision is a cornerstone of rapid reading. The human eye has two distinct regions: the fovea, which is responsible for keen vision, and the peripheral area, which is less sensitive to fine details but can nonetheless detect motion and shapes. Focusing on a single word at a time, or foveal vision, is essential for traditional reading. On the other hand, speed reading teaches readers to focus on the edges of the page rather than the center so they can read more words or lines at once. Moving the focus away from the center of the visual field and onto the periphery can greatly enhance reading speed by decreasing the number of fixations and saccades needed.

The formation of effective patterns of eye movement is another essential component of rapid reading. Instead of the jerky, stop-and-start actions that are typical of normal reading, effective speed readers scan the text with fluid, sweeping gestures. A finger, pen, or pointer can be used in this method, which is also called "meta guiding," to help the eyes move more fluidly across the page. By reducing the possibility of regression or going back to rereading the earlier text, meta-directing helps readers keep to a consistent reading pace.

It is impossible to overstate the importance of cognitive processing when reading quickly. Speed reading strategies aim to improve cognitive processes like comprehension and memory retention, which are essential for effective reading. Chunking is one approach; it entails assembling meaningful pieces of words or phrases. Readers improve their processing speed and memory retention by reading in chunks instead of words. Quicker and more accurate understanding is achieved through chunking by taking advantage of the brain's innate pattern recognition and connection-making abilities.

The mental technique of active reading is another tool for speed readers. Engaging in active reading entails interacting with the text through the use of questions, predictions, and summarizations during the reading process. By actively engaging with the text, comprehension, and memory are strengthened, facilitating information retention and recall. When reading dense or complicated literature, it is very important to adopt active reading techniques so that you can maintain comprehension.

Principles from neurology, especially those pertaining to the brain's processing and storage of information, are also incorporated into the science underlying rapid reading. A number of brain regions, including those involved in visual processing, language comprehension, and memory, are stimulated during reading, according to research. The goal of speed-reading approaches is to improve reading efficiency by maximizing the activation and cooperation of these brain regions. One way to speed up information intake is to decrease subvocalization, which transfers processing power from the auditory to the visual cortex.

The advantages of fast reading are obvious, but you should also be aware of the difficulties and restrictions it presents. When reading complicated or new texts quickly, one of the main complaints leveled against the practice is that it could lead to a loss of understanding and memory. For speed reading to work, the content needs to be simple and familiar so that the reader may use their existing knowledge and context to understand it better. In order to completely understand more difficult texts, it may be required to read them more slowly and deliberately.

Focus and concentration are additional challenges when reading quickly. Reading quickly calls for a high level of focus and mental agility, as any interruptions or changes in attention can ruin your reading session. To keep themselves absorbed in the reading and not miss any crucial details, speed readers need to master the art of attention regulation. Mindfulness and meditation are great ways to sharpen your concentration and focus, which in turn can help you read faster.

One must practice reading at a faster pace while keeping their comprehension level constant in order to become an expert speed reader. Reading quickly is a talent that may be honed with consistent practice. Structured training and exercises are provided by many speed-reading programs and courses to assist individuals in enhancing their skills. Methods for decreasing subvocalization and increasing eye movement efficiency are common components of these programs, as are comprehension assessments and timed reading drills.

The field of rapid reading has benefited from technological developments as well. You can find a variety of speed-reading apps and programs that employ complex algorithms to display information in a manner that improves both reading speed and comprehension. As an example, Rapid Serial Visual Presentation (RSVP) is a method used by some systems. This method involves rapidly flashing words on a screen in a consecutive fashion. Readers can process text more rapidly with RSVP because it decreases eye movements. Users can practice and improve their speed-reading skills with the use of additional tools that include customizable reading speeds, highlighting, and progress monitoring features.

In addition, there are capabilities on e-readers and other digital reading devices that facilitate reading quickly. The reading experience and the ability to read at higher rates can be improved by functions like adjustable font sizes, configurable text layouts, and built-in dictionaries. Additionally, some electronic readers have rapid reading modes that make the material easier to read.

An ideal reading environment, including enough lighting, a lack of distractions, and comfortable seating, is just as important as technical equipment when it comes to speed reading. To aid in the development of speed-reading abilities, it is helpful to establish a regular reading schedule and to define particular reading objectives.

Speed reading has its uses, but it isn't a panacea. It could take some trial and error to figure out which methods and strategies work best for different people. The gains from mastering speed reading can be great and endure for a long time, so it's important to stay patient and keep at it.

To sum up, speed reading is based on scientific principles that optimize the reading process by utilizing several psychological and physiological factors. Improved cognitive processing, less subvocalization, and more efficient eye movement are the goals of speed-reading techniques that are based on an understanding of the interplay between the human brain and the eyes. Reading quickly without sacrificing comprehension or memory is entirely possible with regular practice and the right tactics. Acquiring the skill of speed reading is beneficial since it allows one to save time, be more productive, and gain more knowledge. However, it does have its limitations, especially when reading complicated or unfamiliar literature. Anyone can become an expert speed reader and see the method's transforming power with enough time and effort put into it.

Common Myths and Misconceptions

Since its inception, the skill of speed reading, which is praised for its capacity to improve reading speed and efficiency dramatically, has been surrounded by a great deal of myths and misconceptions. These fallacies are frequently the result of misunderstandings regarding the operation of speed reading and the goals that might be accomplished via its use. Even though speed reading has the potential to be an effective method for rapidly digesting vast amounts of information, it is essential to differentiate between fact and fiction in this practice. This section dives into some of the most widespread fallacies and misunderstandings regarding speed reading, illuminating the truth behind these assertions and elucidating the capabilities and limitations of speed reading.

One of the most common misconceptions regarding speed reading is that it can enable readers to comprehend and assimilate what they read at breakneck speeds, sometimes reaching as high as thousands of words per minute. There is a tendency to exaggerate this claim. Although professional speed readers are indeed able to read at a faster rate than the average person, there is a natural limit to the amount of information that the human brain can digest and be able to comprehend. According to several studies, comprehension tends to decrease as the rate of reading increases beyond a certain threshold. Therefore, although speed reading can improve the efficiency with which one reads, it does not necessarily mean that one can comprehend everything perfectly at extremely fast speeds.

One such widespread misunderstanding is that rapid reading is only skimming through text without actually comprehending what is being read. Skimming and scanning are two techniques that are employed in speed reading. These approaches include swiftly going through text to locate significant information. These techniques are the source of this fallacy. True speed reading, on the other hand, is not about simply skimming over words; rather, it is about teaching the brain to detect and digest bigger amounts of information more effectively. Effective speed-reading techniques are designed to preserve, if not improve, comprehension by fostering active involvement with the content being read.

One misconception related to this is the idea that fast reading can completely do away with the requirement of reading carefully and thoroughly. The reality is that speed reading is a tool that may be utilized selectively based on the surrounding circumstances and the reason for reading. Take, for instance, the practice of speed reading, which is useful for rapidly understanding easy things such as emails, news stories, and other such documents. On the other hand, reading more slowly and deliberately may still be required for more difficult texts that call for a profound comprehension and critical analysis, such as academic papers or literary works. Skill sets such as speed reading and meticulous reading are not mutually exclusive; they complement skills that can be utilized in conjunction with one another.

Additionally, many people need to be made aware that speed reading is a skill that can be learned in a single day or with very little work. This misunderstanding is frequently propelled by marketing and courses that promise outcomes in a short amount of time. Becoming proficient in speed reading calls for regular practice and consistent dedication. The process entails learning various skills, such as reducing subvocalization (the internal voice that occurs during reading), enhancing peripheral vision, and then applying these techniques consistently. Speed reading is a skill that can be improved with time and effort, just like any other skill. To master speed reading, individuals must be patient and persistent in their practice.

In addition, there is a common misconception that speed reading is a universally applicable method that is effective for all individuals. Individuals possess a variety of learning styles, cognitive capacities, and reading preferences; hence, using speed reading strategies is more successful for certain individuals than others. Some people may readily adapt to speed reading methods and notice considerable benefits. Still, some people may need help to break away from traditional reading patterns. Instead of expecting a universal method that would ensure success for everyone, individuals must experiment with numerous techniques and determine what works best for them when it comes to achieving their goals.

Many people think that speed reading is solely about improving the pace at which one reads, with little regard for comprehension and retention. This is a particularly inaccurate misconception. Finding a happy medium between what you read quickly and what you understand is the key to effective speed reading. The objective is not to read as quickly as possible at the expense of comprehension; rather, the objective is to improve reading efficiency by processing material more quickly while still keeping the relevant information for reading. Keeping a high level of comprehension even when reading speed increases can be accomplished through strategies such as chunking, which involves grouping words, employing a pointer to guide the eyes, and practicing active reading.

Many are skeptical of fast reading, arguing that it is either a gimmick or a pseudoscience that has no actual basis in evidence. However, a significant body of research backs up the fundamental concepts that underlie speed reading. Research conducted in the fields of cognitive psychology and neuroscience has shown that the human brain can process visual information at a faster rate than what is generally utilized in traditional reading. The results of studies that investigated eye movements and reading patterns demonstrated that certain strategies, such as lowering the amount of subvocalization and enhancing peripheral vision, can, in fact, result in increased reading rates. A lot of scientific evidence supports speed reading techniques, even though the efficiency of speed reading can differ from person to person.

In addition, there is a common misconception that fast readers never have to go back and reread content or text. To ensure that they have a complete understanding of the content, even the most proficient speed readers may need to review difficult or thick material. It is possible that rereading is a vital component of the learning process since it enables readers to strengthen their understanding and explain any points of uncertainty that they may have seen. Regarding speed reading, the goal is not to avoid rereading but rather to read in such a way that rereading is minimized and becomes more concentrated and meaningful when required.

Additionally, there is a popular belief that speed reading is primarily useful for individuals required to read vast amounts of material, such as students or professionals. Although rapid reading can be especially helpful for certain populations, the applications of this skill are far more widespread. Everyone who wishes to increase their reading efficiency can benefit from speed reading, whether for their delight, self-improvement or to remain informed about current events. One of the most adaptable and valuable tools for people from all walks of life is speed reading since the abilities learned via speed reading can be used in various reading materials and circumstances.

The third fallacy is that taking classes or using technologies designed to improve one's speed of reading is a good use of both time and money. Many respectable programs provide students with essential training and practice to assist them in developing their speed-reading skills. While it is true that not all courses and tools are made equal, there are many programs that offer this sort of assistance. The most important thing is to select programs that are founded on trustworthy scientific ideas and that provide approaches that are both practical and actionable. Investing time and finances in a high-quality speed-reading program can reap considerable dividends when it comes to improving reading speed, comprehension, and general productivity.

When properly used, speed reading is a valuable talent that can improve both the efficiency one reads and the comprehension obtained from reading. However, the myths and misunderstandings that frequently accompany this therapy need to be debunked because they are significant. Speed reading is not a quick-fix solution that can be learned overnight, nor is it a type of reading that involves skimming without absorbing what is being read. To preserve understanding while simultaneously boosting reading speed, engaging in constant practice and taking a balanced approach is necessary. Speed reading techniques offer substantial rewards for those willing to put in the time and effort to develop their skills. These techniques are founded on sound scientific principles, and while they may only work equally well for some, they do offer major benefits. Individuals can make educated judgments about combining these approaches into their reading habits and unlock their full potential if they are thoroughly aware of the facts of speed reading.

CHAPTER II

Identifying and Breaking Bad Reading Habits

Subvocalization: What It Is and How to Overcome It

The practice of mentally "saying" or silently pronouncing words while reading is known as subvocalization. For many people, this behavior is a normal aspect of learning to read and is frequently an instinctive habit formed early in life. Subvocalization greatly slows down reading speed, even if it can help with comprehension and memory. This section will define subvocalization, discuss how it affects reading comprehension, and offer many methods for overcoming it.

The vocal cords and speaking muscles are used during subvocalization, even though no apparent sound is made. This procedure has its roots in the early reading instruction that teaches kids to sound out words. The practice of silently saying words frequently endures as reading ability increases. Subvocalization and auditory processing are tightly related since interpretation in the brain is still facilitated by word sounds. Because it restricts word processing to internal speech speed, which is normally between 150 and 250 words per minute, this dependence might slow down reading.

The principal drawback of subvocalization is its restriction of reading speed. Readers need to utilize their full reading capability when they subvocalize every word they read since the normal speaking pace is far slower than the brain's ability to recognize and interpret words. Subvocalization can be reduced or eliminated to significantly boost efficiency for readers who want to read more, especially in situations when it's necessary to comprehend huge amounts of information rapidly.

Readers can use a variety of strategies to counteract subvocalization by shifting their emphasis from auditory processing to visual and contextual word identification, and pacing oneself while reading is a useful tactic. This might be a pointer, pen, or finger that moves the reader's eyes over the text more quickly than they would otherwise. The brain may be trained to comprehend words visually instead of using the internal auditory loop by making the eyes move faster. This exercise has the potential to lessen the tendency to subvocalize gradually.

Reading in phrases or chunks as opposed to words at a time is another way to reduce subvocalization. This method, also known as chunking, entails identifying word clusters and comprehending the meaning of the cluster as a whole. For instance, a reader might perceive and comprehend "the dog ran quickly" as a unified thought rather than reading it as four separate words. This approach decreases subvocalization while increasing understanding since it concentrates on the whole message instead of specific words.

Seeing the information instead of just saying it out might also aid in lowering subvocalization. Visualization is the process of imagining scenes or pictures in your mind based on the text you are reading. The brain switches from auditory to visual processing—which has the potential to be quicker and more effective—when attention is directed toward visual representations of the information. This method works especially well for narrative or descriptive writings since it makes creating images simple. This talent takes time to master and patience to gain, but it may greatly lessen the habit of subvocalization over time.

Increasing one's vocabulary and linguistic comfort can also help one overcome subvocalization. Readers are more inclined to subvocalize when they come across new terms to guarantee proper pronunciation and comprehension. Increasing one's vocabulary makes it possible to recognize and understand words more quickly without having to say them out. This objective can be met with the assistance of intentional vocabulary-building exercises, exposure to a variety of literature, and regular reading.

Increasing reading speed on purpose is another way to decrease subvocalization. Exercises that include speed reading, such as rapid serial visual presentation (RSVP) and timed reading drills, can teach the brain to digest information more rapidly. For example, RSVP requires the reader to comprehend words or sentences far more quickly than they would otherwise since they are displayed on a screen in rapid succession. Through these activities, readers can learn to read more fluently and rely less on subvocalization to understand what they are reading.

Furthermore, auditory masking is a useful technique for reducing subvocalization. Using this method, you may read while listening to music or background noise. The background noise might lessen the propensity to subvocalize by diverting the brain's attention from silent speech. White noise or instrumental music works especially well since they give aural cues without interfering with the words being read. This technique can be especially helpful in settings when total quiet is not feasible.

Reducing subvocalization can also be accomplished through mindfulness and meditation techniques. These methods facilitate increased concentration and focus, which makes it simpler to pay attention to the text and digest information visually as opposed to audibly. Exercises in mindfulness, such as body scan meditations or attention to the breath, can help teach the mind to remain in the present moment and lessen the inclination to subvocalize. Frequent application of these strategies can improve reading comprehension and general cognitive function.

It's critical to understand that decreasing subvocalization does not mean completely doing away with it. Subvocalization can help with understanding and memory while reading certain kinds of content, such as highly technical or difficult texts. Gaining the ability to decide whether to depend on quicker, more effective reading skills and when to subvocalize is the aim. Through proficiency in various reading approaches, readers may modify their approach according to the nature of the material and their requirements.

Subvocalization needs to be overcome with patience and constant practice. It takes effort to break deeply entrenched reading habits, just like any other. New, more effective reading habits may be formed by scheduling specific times each day for practice with speed reading and applying the previously outlined strategies. Monitoring development and acknowledging incremental advancements can serve as a source of inspiration and support for newly acquired abilities.

Look for resources and assistance in addition to practicing on your own. A plethora of literature, virtual education courses, and computer applications are available to enhance reading comprehension and decrease subvocalization. Participating in forums or reading groups where people exchange advice, anecdotes, and encouragement also offers invaluable accountability and support.

Sustaining optimal physical and mental well-being is essential for proficient reading comprehension and minimizing subvocalization. A good diet, regular exercise, and enough sleep are all important for maintaining cognitive function and focus. Information may be processed and retained more quickly and effectively by a mind that is healthy and well-rested. Additionally, adopting relaxation techniques and stress management might help you stay focused and avoid distractions when reading.

Reducing subvocalization and increasing reading efficiency may both be achieved by approaching the task with a clear purpose and objective in mind. Direction and motivation may be obtained by knowing why you are reading a given material and what knowledge you intend to acquire. Reading with a purpose helps you focus on the information that matters and helps you ignore the rest. This method increases reading comprehension and retention while also increasing reading speed.

It's critical to understand that subvocalization is a prevalent problem that many readers encounter and that perseverance and patience are needed to overcome it.

New reading techniques and habits require patience and persistent work. Celebrating incremental successes and advancements may keep you motivated and boost your self-esteem. Seeking out tools and assistance, like tutors, reading clubs, or internet forums where you can converse with other readers and exchange advice, experiences, and encouragement, is also helpful.

In summary, subvocalization is a normal aspect of reading that might impede the effectiveness and speed of reading. The first step in conquering subvocalization is realizing what it is and how it affects reading. Readers can lessen their need for subvocalization and improve their reading efficiency by applying strategies including using a pacer, chunking, visualizing text, expanding vocabulary, participating in speed reading activities, using auditory masking, and practicing mindfulness. To form new reading habits and improve reading comprehension and speed, one must have patience, perseverance, and a clear goal in mind. Even though it might be difficult to overcome subvocalization, reading more rapidly and efficiently can be achieved with the correct techniques and mentality, making reading more productive and pleasurable.

Regression: Identifying and Reducing Backtracking

Regression, frequently referred to as retracing in the context of reading, is the process of re-reading words, sentences, or entire parts of literature. This behavior can seriously impair reading speed and efficiency, slowing down reading as a whole and possibly lowering comprehension. Reading enjoyment and proficiency can be substantially increased by comprehending the causes of regression and putting reduction techniques into practice.

Many things, such as bad reading habits, limited understanding, and lack of focus, can lead to regression. The reader's lack of confidence in their comprehension of the content is one of the main causes of regression. To make sure they have understood the material, readers frequently go back and re-read passages when they are doubtful. This frequently results in a time-consuming and tedious cycle of reading and re-reading.

Distractions are another frequent reason for regression. It might not be easy to focus when reading in this fast-paced, technologically-driven environment. The reading flow can be interrupted by both internal and external distractions, such as daydreaming or obsessions, as well as noise or interruptions. Readers who have their focus distracted may end up losing their place in the book or missing crucial information, which will force them to go back and re-read it. Regression can also be enhanced and focus reduced when reading in less-than-ideal conditions, such as dimly lit rooms or uncomfortable chairs.

Regression can also result from bad reading habits that have been formed over time. For example, instead of reading a paragraph in a straight line, some readers have a propensity to shift their eyes back and forth across it. Readers may unintentionally re-read passages due to this irregular eye movement. Comparably, reading at a slower pace and having a higher chance of regression can result from subvocalization or the practice of silently pronouncing each word as you read. This is because readers may feel pressured to make sure they have "heard" every word correctly.

Developing ways to improve reading habits, boost comprehension confidence, and improve concentration is critical to effectively reducing regression. Engaging in active reading is one of the best ways to minimize regression. As you read, you should actively engage with the text by posing queries, formulating hypotheses, and summarizing the content. Because readers are more likely to retain and comprehend the information on the first pass, this method not only increases understanding but also decreases the need for backtracking.

Reduction of regression also requires improved concentration. Establishing a comfortable reading space is a crucial phase in this procedure. Selecting a place that is calm, well-lit, and free of distractions will help you stay focused and resist the impulse to go back. Furthermore, establishing clear reading objectives and scheduling regular pauses helps improve focus and ward off mental exhaustion. Since they teach the mind to be present and focused on the work at hand, mindfulness, and meditation techniques can also be helpful.

Enhancing eye movement and visual tracking abilities is another useful method for lowering regression. Utilizing a pacer or guide when reading at a rapid pace helps keep you moving forward and lessens your inclination to go back. A pacer, which can be a finger, pen, or pointer, directs the reader's gaze down the text's lines, promoting a more straightforward and effective reading path. This can help reduce irregular eye movements and the urge to regress by gradually training the eyes to move rapidly and smoothly across the text.

Improving one's vocabulary and prior knowledge can also be very helpful in decreasing regression. Readers are more inclined to go back and check that they have received the content correctly when they come across unfamiliar words or topics. Increasing reading confidence and fluency through the development of a strong vocabulary and subject-matter knowledge base can lessen the need for regression. This objective can be attained through regular reading and exposure to a variety of texts, which acquaint readers with a range of themes, writing styles, and terminologies.

To lessen regression, it's also critical to solve the subvocalization problem. Subvocalization can decrease reading speed and increase the chance of backtracking, even though it can be useful for comprehension in some situations. Readers can practice strategies like reading in phrases rather than single words and concentrating on picturing the text rather than "hearing" it internally to reduce subvocalization. This method lessens the need for regression by encouraging the brain to process words and thoughts more quickly.

Reduction of regression also requires confidence building in reading comprehension. Putting pre-reading techniques into practice is one method to do this. Before beginning a thorough reading, pre-reading entails scanning the text to find the main ideas, headings, and subheadings. It is simpler to learn and retain knowledge during the actual reading process when you have a foundation for understanding the topic from this first overview. Because of this, readers are less likely to doubt their understanding and to go back and read what they have already read.

Reduction of regression and reinforcement of comprehension can also be achieved by note-taking and summary. Summarizing the key points of a document in your own words after reading a chunk of it might help you retain the information and increase understanding. Comparably, making notes while reading can assist in remembering key concepts and points, minimizing the need to go back and read passages again. These procedures not only improve understanding but also serve as a point of reference for upcoming reviews, which lowers the probability of regression even more.

Regression can be minimized and reading efficiency can be increased with intentional training and consistent repetition. Creating a daily routine that includes practicing reading aloud without re-reading helps boost comprehension and confidence. A reasonable challenge can be created by beginning with simpler texts and working your way up to more complicated ones. This will promote continuous improvement. Using resources like reading software and apps can also provide organized practice, track advancement, and give feedback and encouragement to keep improving reading abilities.

Additionally, preserving sound physical and mental health is essential for improving reading comprehension and minimizing regression. Good nutrition, regular exercise, and enough sleep are all important for maintaining cognitive function and focus. Regression is less likely when a mind is in good condition and gets enough sleep, which improves its ability to process and remember information. Additionally, adopting relaxation techniques and stress management might help you stay focused and avoid distractions when reading.

Having a purpose and aim in mind when reading is also beneficial. Knowing why you are reading a given work and the knowledge you expect to acquire might help you stay motivated and on course, which lessens the likelihood that you will revert. Reading with a purpose helps you focus on the information that matters and helps you ignore the rest. This method increases general understanding and retention while also increasing reading efficiency.

It's critical to understand that regression is a typical problem that many readers encounter and that perseverance and patience are needed to overcome it. New reading techniques and habits require patience and persistent work. Celebrating incremental successes and advancements can keep you motivated and boost your self-esteem. Seeking out tools and assistance, like tutors, reading groups, or internet forums where you can converse with other readers and exchange advice, experiences, and encouragement, is also helpful.

To sum up, regression is a major barrier to effective reading that can be overcome and minimized by utilizing a variety of techniques. Readers can create focused strategies to address regression by knowing its causes, which include insufficient comprehension, bad reading habits, and lack of focus. Regression can be minimized by actively reading, focusing better, developing eye movement and visual tracking abilities, increasing vocabulary and background knowledge, limiting subvocalization, and increasing comprehension confidence. Reading satisfaction and efficiency can also be increased by practicing frequently, keeping up good physical and mental health, and approaching the task of reading with a clear goal in mind. Even though regression can be a difficult habit to break, it is possible to attain more effective and efficient reading, which will increase comprehension and help with knowledge retention with the correct tools, patience, and tenacity.

Narrow Vision Span: Expanding Your Field of Vision

The typical problem of narrow vision span, or the restricted field of vision during reading, can have a big effect on understanding and reading speed. This effect happens when readers scan smaller passages of text with each glance instead of focusing on one word or a small number of words at a time. By enabling readers to process more information at once, reading efficiency can be improved by widening the field of vision. This will increase reading speed and comprehension. This section will define restricted vision span, discuss how it affects reading, and go over some methods for enlarging the visual field.

The region of clearest vision in the human eye is called the focus point. This focus usually occurs on one word or a small group of words during reading. Peripheral vision is the term for the area that could be more keen but can still gather information. Because they frequently rely too much on their focal point, readers with limited vision spans read words at a slower pace. This constrained method throws off the text's flow and context, which not only slows down reading but may make it harder to understand.

Training the eyes and brain to process longer text passages at a time is necessary to increase one's field of vision. Readers can improve comprehension and read faster by expanding the area their eyes take in with each glance. Exercises for the eyes that improve peripheral vision are one efficient way to accomplish this. Through these activities, the eyes are trained to move more smoothly and to take in more visual information.

Extending one's field of vision can be achieved by training with letters or numerals arranged in columns. Exercises that show letters or numbers in a column style can be made by readers or found online, and they can then practice reading them quickly without using their eyes. In order to teach the eyes to process more information in a single glance, the objective is to recognize numerous characters at once. With practice, readers can increase their reading speed and range of vision with this activity.

Using a broader reading guide is another way to increase the range of vision. Conventional reading aids, such as a finger or a pen, support direction and focus but frequently promote limited vision by emphasizing just a tiny section of the text. Readers can teach their eyes to read many words at once by using a broader guide, like a card or a ruler. By encompassing a greater area of the text, the broader guide facilitates more fluid and effective eye movement between the lines.

Using fast reading strategies can also aid in increasing one's field of vision. Numerous techniques are used in speed reading in an effort to increase reading speed without sacrificing comprehension. Using a pacer, which moves the eyes along the text lines more quickly, is one such tactic. Readers are compelled to read longer passages of text because the pacer moves quickly, which trains the eyes to focus wider. This exercise can eventually make readers more accustomed to reading at faster rates and with a wider field of view.

Increasing the field of vision can also be facilitated by improving general eye health and function. Frequent eye exercises can improve peripheral vision and develop the eye muscles. Examples of these exercises include practicing eye movements in different directions and focusing on distant things. For optimum reading efficiency, maintaining good eye health through a healthy diet, enough sleep, and frequent eye exams is also crucial. Healthy eyes are better able to absorb information rapidly and effectively, which lessens the pressure and restrictions brought on by limited vision span.

Developing mental techniques is essential for increasing one's field of vision. By using visualization techniques, readers can teach their brains to recognize and digest longer text passages. By visualizing words and sentences in the mind, one can enable the brain to process information more comprehensively than just concentrating on individual words. Reader comprehension and reading speed can both be enhanced by having readers visualize full words or paragraphs. This method works especially well for narrative or descriptive writings because it makes creating imagery simple.

Increasing one's vocabulary and linguistic proficiency can also help one's field of vision. Readers tend to narrow their concentration to ensure correct interpretation when they come across new words. Increasing one's vocabulary makes it easier to recognize and understand words, which makes it possible for readers to read longer passages of text without difficulty. This objective can be attained through regular reading and exposure to a variety of texts, which acquaint readers with a range of themes, writing styles, and terminologies.

Increasing one's field of vision can also be supported by using technology and reading aids. Numerous software applications and apps for speed reading aim to teach readers how to process information more rapidly and effectively. These tools frequently use methods like rapid serial visual presentation (RSVP), which involves rapidly displaying words or phrases on a screen one after the other. Readers can increase their field of vision by using these techniques to educate their eyes and brains to notice and process information more quickly.

Sustaining optimal physical and psychological well-being is essential for proficient reading and widening one's visual sphere. Good nutrition, regular exercise, and enough sleep are all important for maintaining cognitive function and focus. Information can be processed and retained more quickly and effectively by a mind that is healthy and well-rested. Additionally, adopting relaxation techniques and stress management might help you stay focused and avoid distractions when reading.

Reading more efficiently and widening one's field of view can both be achieved by approaching the task with a clear purpose and objective in mind. Direction and motivation can be obtained by knowing why you are reading a given material and what knowledge you intend to acquire. Reading with a purpose helps you focus on the information that matters and helps you ignore the rest. This method increases reading comprehension and retention while also increasing reading speed.

It's critical to understand that broadening the field of vision does not entail completely removing the natural focal point. A more narrowly focused approach can help with comprehension and retention while reading certain kinds of material, such as highly technical or sophisticated reading. The objective is to acquire the adaptability to decide, depending on the kind of content and particular reading requirements, when to rely on a smaller focus and when to widen the field of view. Through experience and familiarity with various reading methods, readers can modify their strategy accordingly.

A narrow visual span can be overcome with patience and persistent practice. It takes time and intentional work to widen one's field of vision, just like any other ability. Building new, more effective reading habits can be facilitated by allocating specific time each day for reading practice and by utilizing the aforementioned strategies. Monitoring development and acknowledging incremental advancements can serve as a source of inspiration and support for newly acquired abilities.

It can be helpful to look for resources and support in addition to practicing on your own. A plethora of literature, virtual education courses, and software applications are available to enhance reading comprehension and broaden one's visual range. Participating in forums or reading groups where people exchange advice, anecdotes, and encouragement can also offer invaluable accountability and support.

Sustaining optimal physical and psychological well-being is essential for proficient reading and widening one's visual sphere. Good nutrition, regular exercise, and enough sleep are all important for maintaining cognitive function and focus. Information can be processed and retained more quickly and effectively by a mind that is healthy and well-rested. Additionally, adopting relaxation techniques and stress management might help you stay focused and avoid distractions when reading.

Reading more efficiently and widening one's field of view can both be achieved by approaching the task with a clear purpose and objective in mind. Direction and motivation can be obtained by knowing why you are reading a given material and what knowledge you intend to acquire.

Reading with a purpose helps you focus on the information that matters and helps you ignore the rest. This method increases reading comprehension and retention while also increasing reading speed.

It is crucial to understand that many readers experience short vision spans and that getting past it takes perseverance and patience. New reading techniques and habits require patience and persistent work. Celebrating incremental successes and advancements can keep you motivated and boost your self-esteem. Seeking out tools and assistance, like tutors, reading groups, or internet forums where you can converse with other readers and exchange advice, experiences, and encouragement, is also helpful.

In conclusion, a mix of measures can be used to address and extend the limited vision span, a substantial barrier to efficient reading. Readers can create focused strategies to address the short vision span by knowing the factors that contribute to it, such as a dependence on focusing vision and bad reading habits. Effective methods for extending the range of vision include doing eye exercises, using broader reading guides, practicing speed reading, enhancing general eye health, applying mental tricks, and leveraging technology. Reading satisfaction and efficiency can also be increased by practicing frequently, keeping up good physical and mental health, and approaching the task of reading with a clear goal in mind. While widening one's field of vision can be difficult, it is possible to read more effectively and efficiently, which improves comprehension and helps retain knowledge if you have the necessary tools, perseverance, and patience.

CHAPTER III

Developing Core Speed Reading Techniques

Skimming and Scanning: Techniques and Applications

For the goal of effectively processing and retrieving information from texts, two key processes in speed reading are known as skimming and scanning. These approaches serve separate objectives and are essential for speed reading. Although both approaches are intended to improve reading efficiency, they are different in terms of how they are implemented or how they are approached. In contrast to scanning, which is a more targeted strategy that aims to identify specific information within a document, skimming includes swiftly moving the eyes over the text in order to acquire a general overview or to understand the key ideas. In this section, we will go into the definitions, techniques, and applications of skimming and scanning. We will also emphasize the benefits of these approaches and provide suggestions for effectively using them.

Skimming is a reading strategy that involves focusing on the essential points of a text without paying attention to the specifics of the text. One of the fundamental objectives of skimming is to recognize the primary concepts, the most important aspects, and the overall organization of the information. When readers need to gain a general idea of the subject or determine its significance before being committed to a comprehensive read, this strategy is particularly effective because it allows them to do both of those things. When time is limited, skimming is frequently used. Some examples of instances in which skimming is utilized include previewing a book, perusing academic articles, or sorting through enormous amounts of material on the internet.

Skimming is a process that calls for the utilization of numerous important tactics. In the first place, it is essential for readers to concentrate on the headers, subheadings, and any language that is highlighted or bolded, as these features often signal information that is of significance. Following that, it is recommended that readers read the introduction and ending paragraphs, as these parts frequently contain a summary of the most important aspects and an overview of the entire manuscript. In addition, it is possible to find essential ideas by reading the first and last phrases of each paragraph. This is because the first and last sentences of each paragraph frequently act as subject sentences, which express the primary idea associated with the paragraph. Readers are able to obtain the key information swiftly and determine whether or not a more extensive read is required if they follow these tactics.

On the other hand, scanning is a method of reading that is utilized to locate particular information that is contained within a text. Scanning is a method of reading that involves looking for specific facts, such as names, dates, numbers, or specific phrases, as opposed to skimming, which is performed with the intention of comprehending the whole text. This method is very helpful for readers who need to locate specific information in a short amount of time, such as when they are looking up a fact in a textbook, locating a quote in an article, or locating a certain section in a document.

To perform scanning effectively, one must have a crystal-clear comprehension of the information that is being searched. It is recommended that readers begin by determining the keywords or phrases that are associated with their search and then proceed to move their eyes over the text in a methodical manner in order to locate these terms. For the purpose of directing the gaze and keeping one's concentration, it is beneficial to make use of visual aids such as a finger or a pen. In addition, being able to recognize text patterns and structures, such as lists, bullet points, or tables, can be of assistance in rapidly locating the information that is sought. By making use of these strategies, readers are able to locate particular data in a straightforward manner without having to read the full text.

Both skimming and scanning offer several advantages to readers, particularly in the information-rich environment of today, where the capacity to process vast volumes of material in a short amount of time is of great value. Skimming enables readers to evaluate the significance and worth of a text before devoting time to a more in-depth reading experience. This reading strategy can help readers save time and increase their productivity. For students and professionals who need to analyze various sources of information and make quick decisions about which books to prioritize, it is very helpful to have this tool.

Scanning, on the other hand, makes it possible for readers to access specific information in a short amount of time, which is essential for activities that require the recovery of data and references in a hurry. All individuals who work with extensive documents or databases, including researchers, journalists, and anyone else, can benefit tremendously from utilizing this technique. It is possible for readers to improve their overall productivity, streamline their workflow, and reduce the amount of time they spend seeking information if they improve their scanning skills.

It is crucial to build and polish the necessary abilities through consistent practice and application in order to include skimming and scanning into reading activities properly. This can be accomplished by means of regular practice. Regularly reviewing different kinds of documents, such as books, academic journals, and newspapers, is one approach to improve skimming. Other forms of literature include academic journals. It is possible for readers to improve their ability to swiftly understand the major concepts and overall structure of various texts by constantly adopting tactics that involve skimming. In a similar vein, readers can improve their ability to locate specifics in a short amount of time by practicing scanning, which involves searching for specific information inside texts. Examples of this include checking definitions, names, or statistics.

When it comes to learning skimming and scanning, one of the most crucial aspects is having a good grasp of when to employ each method. When the objective is to obtain a comprehensive overview or to ascertain the significance of a text, skimming is the most effective method to use. When scanning a list of articles to locate suitable sources for a research paper, for instance, skimming is helpful because it enables the reader to evaluate which articles are most relevant to their topic rapidly. This is an example of how skimming can be very useful. Scanning, on the other hand, is most useful in situations where the goal is to locate particular information. When searching for a certain statistic in a report or looking up a date in a history record, for example, scanning is the most effective method to use.

It is possible for readers to combine the techniques of skimming and scanning with other reading strategies in order to boost the effectiveness of these methodologies further. For instance, skimming a text in order to get a glimpse of what it contains can be followed by a more in-depth reading, during which scanning is utilized to discover and validate particular information found in the text. With this combined method, readers are able first to comprehend the overall content and structure of a text and then efficiently extract specific details whenever they are required to do so from the text.

Skimming and scanning are two techniques that have applications that transcend beyond the realms of academia and the workplace and into everyday life. As an illustration, skimming can be utilized to swiftly analyze emails, news articles, or messages on social media in order to acquire an understanding of the content and significance of these particular items. Searching for a recipe ingredient, looking up information in a user manual, or locating a contact in a phone directory are all examples of situations in which scanning might be considered useful. It is possible for individuals to improve their capacity to efficiently handle and digest information by including skimming and scanning into their everyday reading activities.

Reading strategies such as skimming and scanning can improve not just the efficiency of reading but also the understanding and retention of information. Skimming allows readers to construct a mental framework of the text, which helps them grasp and recall the content of the text. This framework is built by concentrating on the most important concepts and points made in the text. It is possible to reinforce vital information and assure correctness through the process of scanning, which involves directing attention to specific elements. The combination of these strategies results in a well-rounded approach to reading that is beneficial to both reading speed and understanding capacity.

In addition, it is essential to acknowledge that skimming and scanning are not strategies that are incompatible with one another but rather complementary to one another. Effective readers are able to transition between skimming and scanning with ease, depending on the nature of the material they are reading and the goals they have for their reading experience. It is necessary to engage in practice and make a concerted effort to employ the right reading strategy in a variety of reading contexts in order to develop this flexibility. It is possible for readers to develop a more intuitive sense of when to skim for an overview and when to scan for specific information over the course of time, which can lead to significantly improved reading skills overall.

Access to a wide variety of tools and materials is offered in order to facilitate the development of abilities in skimming and scanning. Courses and workshops on speed reading, for instance, sometimes incorporate modules on skimming and scanning, which offer controlled practice and feedback. The exercises and drills that are aimed to improve these techniques can also be found on online platforms and in mobile applications. Additionally, a great number of books and articles on speed reading contain parts on skimming and scanning, which provide readers with advice, tactics, and examples to assist them in improving their overall reading abilities.

When it comes to reading and digesting information in an effective manner, skimming and scanning are two skills that are really necessary. In contrast to scanning, which enables readers to locate specific information swiftly, skimming allows readers to quickly acquire the key concepts and overall structure of a work. Both approaches possess a multitude of advantages, such as the enhancement of comprehension, the acceleration of reading speed, and the enhancement of production. The ability of readers to organize and process huge amounts of information can be considerably improved by the development and refinement of abilities in skimming and scanning through consistent practice and application. It is possible to further improve the effectiveness of these reading methods by gaining an understanding of when and how to utilize each strategy, as well as by merging them with other reading strategies. Mastering the skills of skimming and scanning can lead to improved reading ability and a more effective method of managing information, regardless of whether the context is academic, professional, or ordinary.

Using a Pointer: Benefits and Methods

Reading with a pointer, often known as "pointer reading," is a method that includes directing the eyes down lines of text with a physical item, such as a finger, pen, or another similar device. This technique is sometimes referred to as "pointer reading." This technique has been utilized for centuries and continues to be applicable in the present day, particularly with regard to the enhancement of reading comprehension and the speed with which one can read. The utilization of a pointer can result in a multitude of advantages, such as greater concentration, increased reading speed, and higher understanding. The purpose of this section is to investigate the numerous advantages of utilizing a pointer when reading, as well as the various approaches and strategies that may be utilized to incorporate this practice successfully.

When reading, having a pointer is beneficial for a number of reasons, but one of the most important ones is that it helps maintain attention and concentration. While reading, particularly lengthy or complicated texts, it is simple for the eyes to wander or for the mind to become distracted. This is especially true when reading. The use of a pointer offers a tactile guide that leads the eyes along the lines of text, so lowering the possibility of losing one's position and eliminating distractions. This heightened concentration can result in a more immersive reading experience, which in turn enables the reader to establish a more profound connection with the subject matter. A pointer can also aid in synchronizing eye movements by physically directing the eyes, which provides a smoother and more constant reading flow. This is because the pointer physically guides the eyes.

In addition to improving one's ability to concentrate, the use of a pointer can considerably increase one's reading speed. People who regularly engage in the practice of rapid reading will benefit tremendously from this especially. The reader is encouraged to move their eyes over the text at a faster rate by the pointer, which acts as a pacemaker. The use of the pointer helps to prevent the eyes from lingering on specific words or phrases, which can slow down the reading process. This is accomplished by maintaining a consistent pace on the page. This exercise has the potential to educate the eyes to move more fluidly and effectively over time, which can ultimately lead to an improvement in reading speed throughout the population. Another aspect that might slow down reading speed is subvocalization, which is the practice of silently pronouncing words in one's thoughts while reading. The usage of a pointer can assist in minimizing subvocalization, which is a habit that can be reduced by using a pointer.

One other advantage of employing a pointer is that it has the potential to boost both understanding and the ability to remember important information. When readers make use of a pointer, they are more likely to remain engaged with the material, which ultimately results in improved comprehension and information retention. Maintaining a regular reading rhythm is made easier with the aid of the pointer, which might improve one's ability to comprehend the general structure and flow of the course content. Furthermore, readers are able to absorb better and digest the material that is being read if they keep their attention and minimize distractions within their environment. Students and professionals who need to retain a significant quantity of knowledge efficiently will find this to be a very helpful tool.

There are a variety of approaches and strategies that may be utilized in order to make optimal use of a pointer when reading. The use of a finger as a pointer is, without a doubt, one of the most straightforward and widespread approaches. Because it assists young children in tracking the text and developing early reading abilities, this method is frequently taught to young children when they are first starting to read. To make advantage of this technique, readers need to position their index finger beneath the line of text that they are now reading and then move it in a smooth motion along the line. Eyes are guided and attention is maintained with the aid of this. Although pointing with a finger is an efficient method, it can occasionally obscure the view of the text. For this reason, some readers choose to use other items as pointers instead of their fingers.

It is common practice to use a pen or pencil as an alternative to using one's finger. This strategy offers the same advantages of directing the eyes and keeping the attention, but it does so without blocking the text. In order for readers to utilize a pen or pencil as a pointer, they must grip the object in their dominant hand and position the tip of the object slightly below the line of text. A constant movement of the pen or pencil along the line is something that they do when they are reading. It is very helpful for speed reading since the pen or pencil may be moved swiftly and smoothly across the text, which encourages quicker eye movements. This approach is particularly good for speed reading.

Utilizing a ruler or a straight edge is just another efficient technique for highlighting an area. It is especially helpful for readers who need help sustaining a constant reading flow or who need help holding their position in the text. This approach is especially effective for those readers. Readers have the ability to utilize a ruler as a pointer by positioning the edge of the ruler just below the line of text that they are now reading and then moving it down the page as they continue reading. The text that has already been read is covered, which helps reduce the urge to go back and read it again. This not only helps lead the eyes, but it also helps cover the text. Because it offers straightforward and consistent guidance, this technique can be very useful for people who struggle with reading, such as those who have dyslexia or other reading issues.

The pointer technique is incorporated into specialist reading equipment and software, which are accessible to individuals who want a more advanced way of reading. By replicating the impact of a physical pointer, digital reading aids, such as e-readers and reading apps, frequently incorporate capabilities that enable users to highlight text or follow a moving cursor. These features let users read more efficiently. In order to accommodate the tastes and requirements of each individual reader, these tools may be adjusted to modify the pace and style of the pointer. Additionally, some speed-reading software offers guided reading modes. In these modes, a moving bar or highlighter directs the eyes across the text at a predefined rate. This allows readers to practice and improve their reading speed as well as their comprehension.

Reading exercise that includes the use of a pointer can also have positive effects on cognitive development. Through the utilization of a pointer, several senses are stimulated, resulting in the combination of visual and kinesthetic input, which has the potential to improve cognitive processing and memory retention. A multimodal experience is created for readers when they physically guide their eyes with a pointer. This experience has the potential to strengthen brain pathways that are related to reading and understanding. Due to the fact that it offers extra stimuli to promote focus and engagement with the text, this multisensory method can be especially effective for persons who have both learning difficulties and attention issues.

In order to get the most of the advantages that come with utilizing a pointer, it is essential to practice using it on a regular basis and to create consistency in how you use it. The acquisition of pointer reading skills needs time and effort, just like the acquisition of any other talent. Readers should begin by applying the pointer approach to texts that are already familiar and comfortable to them. As they become more proficient, they should progressively increase the level of difficulty and length of the content they are reading. Using a pointer can become more intuitive and natural over time if you consistently use it. This is because consistent repetition will assist in creating muscle memory and eye coordination.

While the use of a pointer can considerably improve reading efficiency and comprehension, it is important to remember that it may not be appropriate for all types of reading or for all persons. This is something that should be taken into consideration. For instance, readers who usually engage with books that are extremely technical or thick may discover that the pointer approach is less successful. This is because these types of texts typically need a slower and more deliberate reading pace. Individuals who have already evolved a reading style that is very efficient and successful would likely not find considerable gains from employing a pointer. In the same way that it is vital to consider personal preferences and reading goals while determining whether or not to include a pointer into one's reading practice, it is also important to consider any other reading approach.

In addition to improving reading speed and comprehension, employing a pointer has a number of other advantages. Making the reading experience more participatory and interesting is another way that this method may improve the overall quality of the reading experience. A sense of active engagement in the reading process may be created by the gesture of physically directing the eyes with a pointer. This can lead to an increase in both motivation and enjoyment of the reading experience. Employing a pointer may make reading feel more dynamic and interesting for young readers and pupils, which can contribute to the development of a love of reading that will last a lifetime.

The pointer approach has the potential to be a very helpful tool for educators and teachers working in educational environments. For the purpose of assisting kids in the development of early reading abilities such as tracking and attention, instructors might introduce students to the usage of a pointer. Students who have trouble retaining focus or who struggle with reading fluency may benefit tremendously from utilizing this method with great potential. In addition, the pointer approach may be utilized in group reading activities. In these activities, students take turns using a pointer to guide the class through a book, which encourages collaborative learning and participation.

To summarize, the utilization of a pointer while reading has several advantages, such as the enhancement of concentration, the enhancement of reading speed, and the improvement of understanding. By assisting in the maintenance of attention, the reduction of distractions, and the alignment of the eyes along lines of text, the pointer approach contributes to the creation of a reading experience that is more efficient and effective. The use of this strategy in reading practice may be accomplished by the utilization of a variety of instruments, including the use of a finger, pen, pencil, ruler, or digital tools. When it comes to establishing skills with pointer reading, consistent repetition and regular practice are essential components. Additionally, the cognitive benefits of using many senses can further boost understanding and memory retention. Despite the fact that the pointer approach might not be appropriate for all forms of reading or for all persons, it is an extremely helpful tool for people who are trying to enhance their reading abilities and their entire reading experience. Within educational settings as well as in other contexts, the pointer technique has the potential to cultivate a love of reading and to encourage the formation of good reading habits. This is accomplished by making reading more interactive and engaging.

Chunking: Reading Groups of Words

Chunking, which is the process of organizing words into meaningful groups or "chunks," is an effective way to increase reading comprehension and efficiency. By making use of the brain's capacity for segmented processing, this method can greatly improve comprehension of difficult texts and reading speed. Chunking has its origins in cognitive psychology and is frequently used in a variety of settings, such as reading, learning, and remembering. This section examines chunking in the context of reading, going over its advantages, underlying principles, and practical application techniques.

Fundamentally, chunking is the technique of dividing a text into digestible, easily remembered chunks. Readers arrange words into phrases or clusters that communicate a single idea or piece of information, as opposed to reading each word separately. This approach takes use of the brain's innate propensity to divide information into manageable chunks, which improves cognitive efficiency. Readers can lessen the cognitive load and free up their brains to concentrate on understanding instead of reading comprehension skills by chunking.

Reading chunking has several advantages. Reading more quickly is one of the biggest benefits. Reading becomes slower when readers concentrate on individual words because their eyes scan the text more slowly and more often. Chunking decreases the amount of eye movements and speeds up reading by enabling the eyes to scan more words in a single glance. Those who must swiftly comprehend big amounts of text, such as professionals and students, would especially benefit from this speed increase.

Chunking not only increases speed but also enhances comprehension. Words may be organized into meaningful pieces that help readers better comprehend the context and connections between concepts. By reading the book holistically, one can better understand its general meaning rather than being mired in its particular words. Since the brain is more likely to recall related information in chunks rather than individual words, chunking also helps with knowledge retention. This enhanced retention is particularly helpful in professional and academic contexts where the capacity to remember and apply knowledge is essential.

The working memory and information processing capacities of the brain constitute the foundation of the cognitive mechanisms behind chunking. Working memory is only able to store and process data for brief intervals of time. Chunking makes the most of this capability by dividing data into more understandable, bigger chunks. This method makes use of the brain's capacity for pattern recognition and connection-making, which promotes effective information processing and storage. Chunking improves reading efficiency by allowing the brain to handle more information at once by lowering the number of discrete units that must be processed.

Using chunking in reading instruction requires a number of methods and approaches. Starting with well-known and simple books and advancing to increasingly complicated material as competency increases is a useful strategy. To start, readers can recognize the text's natural breaks—phrases, clauses, and sentences—and practice reading these passages aloud in chunks. For instance, a reader could chunk the line "The quick brown fox jumps over the lazy dog" into "The quick brown fox" and "jumps over the lazy dog" rather than reading it word for word. This technique aids in the formation of the habit of classifying words and identifying significant units.

Using visual cues to identify textual sections, such as underlining or highlighting, is another chunking strategy. Readers may practice reading the grouped words as a single unit and concentrate on them with the aid of this graphic depiction. When they gain proficiency in identifying and cognitively processing chunks, they will be able to decrease their dependence on visual aids over time. Furthermore, chunking practice with a variety of texts— including fiction, non-fiction, and technical material—can help readers become more flexible and modify the strategy for varied reading situations.

Enhancing one's vocabulary and knowledge with linguistic structures can also help one become more adept at chunking. A large vocabulary makes it easier for readers to comprehend and recognize words faster, which makes it easier to combine words into chunks. Understanding popular phrases, idioms, and grammatical structures helps readers recognize word relationships and form natural groups. These abilities may be developed via consistent reading and exposure to a variety of books, which will make chunking a more natural and efficient technique.

Chunking can be used in conjunction with fast reading strategies to increase its advantages. Chunking is a fundamental element of many speed-reading techniques. Speed reading encompasses a variety of tactics intended to accelerate reading speed while preserving understanding. A pacer, such as a finger or pen, can be used, for instance, to help direct the eyes along text passages and keep the reading rate consistent. Chunking words rapidly and effectively may also be developed by practicing with speed reading drills, such as timed reading exercises and rapid serial visual presentation (RSVP).

Digital tools and technology can offer extra assistance with chunking. Software and applications for speed reading frequently have functions that highlight or aggregate words into manageable pieces, enabling users to practice the method in an organized and engaging way. The size and tempo of the chunks may be changed with these tools to suit the preferences and ability level of each reader. A visual tool for chunking practice is also provided by certain e-readers and digital platforms that enable users to comment and mark textual portions.

Chunking has advantages, but it also has drawbacks. One typical challenge is the inability to recognize natural chunks, particularly in technical or dense literature. Some readers could find it difficult to identify significant word clusters, which could result in reading that needs to be more coherent or uninterrupted. It's crucial to practice chunking with a range of texts in order to overcome this difficulty, and you may also ask teachers or reading resources for advice. Building competence can also be facilitated by segmenting complicated texts into smaller, easier-to-read chunks and progressively increasing the chunk size.

Maintaining understanding while using chunking to increase reading speed presents another difficulty. It's possible that some readers will discover that reading quickly compromises their comprehension of the content. To solve this problem, it's critical to find a balance between comprehension and quickness. While chunking to boost speed, active reading techniques like summarizing, asking, and making predictions can help cement comprehension. Readers can also improve their ability to chunk words quickly and maintain comprehension with regular practice and feedback.

Teachers and educators often find chunking to be a useful technique in educational contexts. Students' reading abilities can be enhanced and their overall academic performance can be raised by introducing them to the idea of chunking and offering guided practice. Chunking can offer younger students—or those who are struggling with reading—a disciplined and doable method of absorbing material. To reinforce the method and make learning interesting and successful, teachers can employ a variety of activities, including interactive reading games, group reading exercises, and chunk highlighting.

Chunking is used in reading, but it also has wider effects on memory and learning. The method is frequently utilized to improve knowledge processing and retention in a variety of domains, including educational psychology, cognitive psychology, and language acquisition. Chunking is a useful technique for both professionals and students since it increases learning efficiency and effectiveness by grouping knowledge into coherent parts. Gaining an understanding of chunking concepts and using them in various situations can enhance cognitive function and increase one's chances of success in both academic and professional endeavors.

Chunking is an effective strategy that may greatly improve reading memory, comprehension, and efficiency. Readers can improve comprehension of difficult texts, decrease cognitive load, and read faster by organizing words into meaningful units. By utilizing the brain's capacity for pattern recognition and information organization, chunking's cognitive mechanisms maximize working memory and information processing. Using chunking in reading practice comprises a number of tactics, including beginning with well-known books, making use of visual aids, expanding vocabulary, and using speed reading methods. Although there are barriers to overcome, readers may become proficient and overcome them with consistent practice and supervised teaching. Chunking is a useful technique for professionals, students, and anybody else looking to enhance their cognitive function because of its wide range of advantages that go beyond reading to include learning and memory applications.

Leisure Reading and Continuous Learning

When leisure reading and continual learning are combined, they provide a potent combination that fosters lifelong curiosity, mental development, and intellectual advancement. The voluntary act of reading literature, fiction, non-fiction, or any other kind of written material that interests the reader without the burden of academic or professional commitments is referred to as leisure reading or reading for pleasure. On the other side, continuous learning refers to the lifelong pursuit of information and abilities. Together, these approaches promote a culture of lifelong learning and intellectual curiosity that goes well beyond traditional schooling. This section examines the connection between leisure reading and ongoing education, stressing the advantages of both, the ways in which they foster professional and personal development and practical ways to incorporate both into everyday life.

Numerous social, emotional, and cognitive advantages come from leisure reading. It improves vocabulary, understanding, and critical thinking abilities on a cognitive level. People who read for enjoyment are exposed to a large vocabulary and intricate sentence patterns, which might help them become more proficient in language and increase their understanding. Individuals can explore a variety of genres and topics at their own speed with leisure reading, in contrast to structured learning, which frequently focuses on specified results. Having the choice to select what to read encourages a love of books and an innate desire to learn, which results in a more in-depth and meaningful interaction with the subject matter.

Leisure reading has emotional benefits such as lowering stress, improving empathy, and offering a sense of escape. Getting lost in a good book may be a very effective stress-relieving strategy that provides a little reprieve from the stresses of everyday life. Studies have indicated that reading can result in a calmer state of mind by lowering heart rates and reducing muscular tension. Moreover, reading fiction, in particular, helps improve empathy because it lets readers see the world from the viewpoints of other characters. One of the most important aspects of emotional intelligence, which is essential for both personal and professional interactions, is the capacity to comprehend and share the sentiments of others.

Reading for pleasure can promote social interactions and dialogue. Books are a great starting point for talks, whether they take place in book clubs, online discussion boards, or informally with friends and family. Readers may form a feeling of community and establish social ties by exchanging ideas and observations about books. Reading works by a variety of authors and genres may also introduce readers to other people's experiences, perspectives, and cultures, which can increase their cultural sensitivity and awareness.

In today's world of fast change, continuous learning—the pursuit of information and skills beyond formal education—becomes indispensable. People need to continuously upgrade their knowledge and skills in order to be competitive, given the speed at which technology is developing and the changing nature of the employment market. Numerous resources are available for continuous learning, such as workshops, online learning environments, professional development courses, and self-directed study. It is motivated by a growth mentality, which is the conviction that aptitude and intellect can be enhanced by commitment and diligence.

The efficiency of lifetime learning initiatives may be greatly increased by including leisure reading in continuous learning. By encouraging a curious and open-minded perspective, leisure reading promotes lifelong learning. People who read for enjoyment are more inclined to investigate subjects outside of their immediate area of expertise, which increases their knowledge base and promotes interdisciplinary thinking. This thought exchange may result in fresh viewpoints and creative solutions, which are beneficial in both personal and professional settings.

Furthermore, reading for pleasure may enhance professional growth and formal education by giving theoretical knowledge context and depth. While leisure reading enables a more comprehensive and nuanced comprehension of issues, formal learning frequently concentrates on certain skills or information. Reading historical fiction, for instance, may offer readers an understanding of historical occurrences and civilizations that are only sometimes included in textbooks. In a similar vein, reading popular science and scientific literature may make difficult scientific ideas easier to comprehend and more interesting for readers. Enhancing critical thinking and problem-solving abilities is possible with this deeper comprehension, which is crucial for lifelong learning.

The advantages of incorporating recreational reading into ongoing education are not limited to a single profession. Reading about leadership, organizational behavior, and innovation in business and management, for instance, may offer insightful information and motivation. Books with in-depth analyses and case studies, such as Clayton Christensen's "The Innovator's Dilemma" and Jim Collins' "Good to Great," can help in strategic planning and decision-making. Healthcare practitioners may remain up to speed on developing trends and best practices in the area of medicine by reading about the latest research and advancements in books and medical journals. Teachers who read for pleasure may promote a culture of inquiry and lifelong learning in their pupils by bringing new ideas and views into the classroom.

People can use a variety of tactics to incorporate leisure reading into ongoing education successfully. First of all, making time in one's schedule for reading every day might aid in creating a habit and integrating reading into daily life. Over time, even 15 to 30 minutes a day of reading can result in notable cognitive improvements. The experience of reading may also be improved by setting up a distraction-free, comfortable reading space. This might involve creating a cozy reading area, providing adequate lighting, and reducing technological device disruptions.

Second, reading a variety of books helps extend one's perspective and pique one's intellectual interest. This can contain historical books, science fiction, fiction, non-fiction, biographies, and more. Reading works by various authors and genres may introduce readers to fresh concepts, viewpoints, and civilizations, which can broaden their perspective on the world. Participating in book clubs or virtual reading communities can yield prospects for conversation and idea sharing, augmenting the recreational and educational advantages of reading.

Third, combining reading with other educational activities might result in a more comprehensive and richer education. Combining reading with writing, for instance, by creating book reviews or maintaining a reading diary, can improve understanding and memory. Engaging in dialogues may enhance learning by giving one a chance to express and defend their opinions, whether in online forums or book clubs. Furthermore, going to literary festivals, author talks, and book-related events may give you a greater understanding of the works and the creative processes that went into them.

Additionally, technology may be a big help for ongoing education and pleasure reading. Different tastes and lives may be accommodated by the handy and accessible reading options offered by e-readers, audiobooks, and online libraries. With the potential to hold thousands of volumes, e-readers have the benefit of mobility, making it simple to take a library with you everywhere you go. For people who would rather listen than read, audiobooks offer a substitute, and they may be listened to while exercising, traveling, or engaging in other activities. A wide range of books and materials are available through digital reading platforms and online libraries, sometimes at a lesser price than traditional books.

Additionally, by offering extra resources and learning opportunities, educational websites and online learning platforms may enhance leisure reading. Courses in a variety of subjects are available on websites such as Coursera, edX, and Khan Academy, which enables people to enhance their knowledge and abilities in areas of interest. In order to support students in delving further into a subject, a lot of these sites also offer reading lists and suggested books. Reading for pleasure, along with online education, can help people build a rich and varied learning environment that fosters lifelong learning.

The advantages of ongoing learning and leisure reading extend beyond personal development to have wider social ramifications. A culture that places a high importance on reading and lifelong learning is better able to handle difficult problems and adjust to change. Reading fosters empathy and critical thinking, two qualities necessary for knowledgeable and caring citizenship. A culture of creativity and flexibility is fostered by continuous learning and is essential for both social and economic advancement. Societies may develop more informed, involved, and resilient citizens by promoting leisure reading and lifelong learning.

Promoting leisure reading and lifelong learning can have a significant positive effect on student's academic and personal growth in school settings. Students can develop a passion for reading and a habit of lifetime learning by being encouraged to read for pleasure. By offering a varied and well-stocked library, integrating leisure reading into the curriculum, and planning reading-related events and activities, schools may help with this. By sharing their own reading recommendations and experiences, as well as by fostering a reading-loving environment in the classroom, teachers may serve as role models for students.

Promoting a culture of continual learning at work can improve worker engagement, output, and creativity. By granting access to resources for professional development, encouraging attendance at seminars and courses, and fostering a growth attitude, employers may encourage continual learning. Providing avenues for staff members to exchange their knowledge and perspectives, such as organizing study circles or lunch-and-learn sessions, may also promote a cooperative and intellectually engaging workplace.

Reading for pleasure and continuing education are two complementary activities that can greatly promote lifetime curiosity, mental health, and intellectual development. Reading for pleasure has social, emotional, and cognitive benefits that promote a love of books and an innate desire to learn. In today's world of fast change, a growth mindset is crucial for continuous learning, which supports the never-ending quest for information and skills. Including recreational reading in ongoing education may extend perspectives, boost comprehension, and promote both professional and personal development. People may successfully integrate leisure reading into their lives by using techniques including making time for reading, choosing a variety of reading materials, and combining reading with other learning activities. This integration may be strengthened by technology and online learning environments, which offer easily accessible and practical reading and learning options. Reading for pleasure and lifelong learning have advantages that go beyond personal development and have wider social ramifications. They foster creativity, empathy, and critical thinking. By promoting these behaviors in both educational and professional environments, we may foster a society that is more informed, involved, and resilient.

CHAPTER IV

Tools and Technologies for Speed Reading

Speed Reading Software and Apps

In recent years, there has been a noticeable surge in the popularity of speed-reading applications and software, which are solutions meant to assist people in reading more quickly without sacrificing or even improving comprehension. The capacity to read rapidly and effectively increases in value as our modern lifestyle quickens and the amount of information we must comprehend expands. These digital tools are appealing to professionals, students, and lifelong learners alike since they use a range of strategies based on the principles of speed reading to enable quicker reading. This section examines the characteristics, advantages, and possible disadvantages of applications and software for rapid reading, as well as how they affect learning objectives and reading habits.

Numerous strategies are employed by speed reading applications and software to assist users in increasing their reading speed. Quick Serial Visual Presentation (RSVP), which includes showing words or phrases one at a time in quick succession at a fixed area on the screen, is one of the most popular techniques. By using this approach, reading speed can be increased since less time is spent shifting the eyes back and forth across the page. RSVP's word presentation speed may be altered, enabling users to progressively pick up the pace of reading as they get more accustomed to the method.

Chunking is another common method employed by speed reading software, in which the text is split up into chunks of words or phrases so that the reader may comprehend many words at once. This approach makes use of the brain's innate capacity to identify patterns and cluster relevant data, which speeds up understanding. Additionally, several applications employ guided reading techniques—like underlining or highlighting text—to assist users in staying on task and lessen the chance of regression or the practice of reading material again.

Another element that is frequently incorporated in speed reading software is eye movement exercises. By training the eyes to travel more quickly over the text, these exercises aim to lessen fixations and saccades, which are fast eye movements that can impede reading speed. These exercises can assist users in creating a more fluid and effective reading style by enhancing eye coordination and minimizing pointless motions.

Comprehending assessments and progress monitoring features are frequently included in speed-reading applications and software. These tools aid users in evaluating their comprehension of the subject matter and pinpointing areas in need of development. After a reading session, comprehension assessments usually entail answering questions on the text and offering quick feedback on how well the reading strategies being used are working. Reading speed, comprehension scores and other metrics may be tracked over time using tracking tools, which enables users to track their development and modify their training as necessary.

There are several advantages to utilizing apps and software for rapid reading. The potential for huge time savings is one of the biggest benefits. People may digest more information in less time by reading faster, which is especially helpful for professionals who must keep current in their professions, students who have a lot of reading to do, and anybody who loves to read for pleasure but finds it difficult to find the time. Enhanced efficiency has the potential to result in higher production and the capacity to cope with the continuous flow of information in the current digital era.

The possible increase in retention and comprehension is an additional advantage. Many speed-reading programs place a strong emphasis on the value of comprehension, despite some detractors who claim that speed reading trades comprehension for speed. These programs improve comprehension by assisting readers in concentrating on the general meaning of the text rather than becoming bogged down by individual words. Examples of these strategies include chunking and guided reading. Furthermore, consistent use of speed-reading software can educate the brain to digest information more rapidly and efficiently, which may enhance memory and recall of the content.

Software and applications for speed reading can help improve mental agility and cognitive flexibility. The ability to digest and interpret material quickly forces the brain to change and create new neural connections, which can enhance cognitive performance in general. Beyond improving reading comprehension, this cognitive training may also improve critical thinking, problem-solving abilities, and the speed at which new knowledge may be processed and assimilated.

There are potential disadvantages and restrictions to consider, in addition to the numerous advantages. The caliber and efficacy of certain speed-reading programs is one issue. The quality and rigor of the applications and software available for fast reading vary widely. Certain systems could overstate their promise for much faster reading without placing enough focus on understanding. Users should make sure they are selecting a reliable and efficient tool by carefully weighing the features and reviews of various apps.

The possibility of being a shallow reader is another possible disadvantage. Some users may emphasize speed above comprehension depth in their quest for quicker reading rates, which results in a more superficial interaction with the material. This can be especially troublesome when dealing with intricate or subtle content that calls for in-depth thought and contemplation. Users must maintain a deep and meaningful engagement with the topic while balancing their fast reading practice with more thoughtful and contemplative reading periods in order to reduce this danger.

Furthermore, not all kinds of reading material will work with rapid reading applications or software. While these technologies can be very useful for digesting enormous amounts of text, like reports, articles, and non-fiction novels, they might not be as useful for reading literary works like poetry, fiction, or other works that call for a more involved and emotional reading experience. It's possible for readers to discover that some books are better read slowly, which makes for a deeper, more reflective reading experience.

Apps and software for rapid reading can have a big influence on learning objectives and reading habits. These technologies have the power to change how many people read, increasing its effectiveness and enjoyment. Users may broaden their knowledge base and remain up to date with new advances in their areas of interest by improving their reading comprehension and speed. More success in school and the workplace, as well as an educated and involved attitude to lifetime learning, can result from this.

Additionally, using applications and software for speed reading can encourage a growth attitude and a dedication to ongoing development. The ability to read quickly calls for commitment, endurance, and a readiness to step beyond one's comfort zone. Through goal-setting, progress monitoring, and milestone celebration, users may cultivate a sense of achievement and drive to improve their reading abilities further. This growth attitude may be applied to other facets of life as well, promoting a proactive and resilient method of developing oneself and one's career.

Apps and software for fast reading can be useful resources for teachers and students in educational settings. With the aid of these resources, students may enhance their understanding and retention, manage extensive reading lists, and acquire critical study techniques. Teachers may boost students' reading development and promote an efficient and successful learning culture by integrating speed reading programs into their curricula. Additionally, by offering specialized activities and strategies to enhance reading comprehension and fluency, speed reading aids can help kids with learning disabilities, such as dyslexia.

Apps and software for rapid reading can improve worker productivity and career advancement in the office. The capacity to absorb and understand vast amounts of information rapidly may be a big advantage in fields like law, finance, and healthcare, where remaining educated and current is essential. By granting access to speed reading tools and promoting their usage as part of continuing professional development activities, employers may assist in their workers' development. Organizations may improve overall performance and competitiveness by cultivating a culture of efficiency and continual learning.

Setting goals, practicing frequently, and taking a balanced approach to reading will help you incorporate speed reading applications and software into your everyday life. To begin, users can spend a specific period of time each day to practicing speed reading strategies, progressively accelerating their reading speed and content complexity. A sense of direction and motivation may be gained by setting concrete objectives, such as finishing a given number of comprehension exams or increasing reading speed by a specified percentage.

A healthy balance between rapid reading and more contemplative reading techniques must also be maintained. While reading quickly may be a very useful strategy for absorbing a lot of information, it's equally critical to take the time to connect with more complicated or emotionally charged content fully. By using a balanced approach, readers may benefit from improved reading comprehension and speed while still maintaining a meaningful and enjoyable reading experience.

The usefulness and accessibility of applications and software for rapid reading are greatly influenced by technology. These tools are now more accessible than ever thanks to developments in digital platforms and mobile technology, which enable users to practice speed reading while on the go and easily incorporate it into their regular routines. Convenient platforms for speed reading applications include e-readers, tablets, and smartphones. These devices provide customizable features such as text size, backdrop color, and reading speed to meet the tastes and requirements of individual users.

Furthermore, the advancement of machine learning and artificial intelligence may significantly increase the efficacy of fast-reading software. Real-time feedback, adaptive learning pathways, and tailored recommendations are just a few of the features that AI-driven solutions offer to help users maximize their practice and more successfully meet their reading objectives. In addition to analyzing reading habits and pinpointing problem areas, these technologies may also provide focused workouts and techniques to increase comprehension and reading speed.

In conclusion, a variety of features and advantages are provided by speed reading applications and software, which may greatly improve reading comprehension and efficiency. To assist people in reading more quickly without losing comprehension, strategies including chunking, RSVP, guided reading, and eye movement exercises are employed. These technologies provide time savings, better recall and understanding, and more cognitive flexibility. It is important to do a thorough assessment of the caliber and efficacy of various initiatives and to strike a balance between rapid reading and more contemplative reading techniques. Speed reading applications and software have an influence on daily life, business, and educational environments by encouraging a culture of efficiency and lifelong learning. The prospect of ever more individualized and efficient speed-reading tools presents promising opportunities for the development of reading and education in the future as technology progresses. People may build vital abilities that promote academic and professional success, as well as a lifetime enjoyment of reading and learning, by including speed reading exercises in their daily routines.

E-Readers and Digital Tools

The way we read, study, and access information has been completely transformed by e-readers and digital technologies. Numerous advantages are provided by these devices, including improved reading experiences, portability, accessibility, and ease. E-readers and other digital tools become more and more capable as technology develops, which makes them essential for contemporary education, career advancement, and personal enrichment. The present discourse delves into the diverse attributes, advantages, and obstacles linked to e-readers and digital tools, scrutinizing their influence on reading behaviors, educational achievements, and the community at large.

Electronic devices called e-readers are made expressly to read digital books, periodicals, and other written materials. Popular e-readers with high-resolution screens, intuitive user interfaces, and vast digital libraries, like the Kobo, Nook, and Kindle from Barnes & Noble and Amazon, have become increasingly popular. Compared to conventional backlit screens, e-ink technology, which imitates the appearance of ink on paper, lessens eye strain in these gadgets. A variety of features, such as changeable font sizes, customized backdrops, integrated dictionaries, and note-taking capabilities, are available on e-readers to improve the reading experience.

The mobility of e-readers is one of their main benefits. Thousands of books may be stored on an e-reader, which means you no longer need to carry along many physical books. For frequent readers, students, and travelers who value having access to their complete library at all times, this convenience is especially beneficial. E-readers are also portable and lightweight, which makes it simple to carry them in a pocket or backpack.

An additional noteworthy advantage of e-readers is their accessibility. Readers no longer have to go to a real library or bookshop to get a wide variety of information because digital books can be downloaded quickly from websites, bookstores, and other sources. Since physical books may be hard to come by in isolated or underdeveloped places, this rapid access to information is quite helpful. Additionally, e-readers are equipped with features like text-to-speech capabilities, changeable text sizes, and screen readers that help those who have visual impairments or reading challenges.

A vast array of digital tools and software are available to enhance reading and learning in addition to e-readers. Digital material may be read on tablets and smartphones that have e-reading programs like Google Play Books,

Apple Books, and Kindle installed. The ability to connect to the internet gives these devices an extra benefit, allowing users to engage with multimedia material, download new books, and access online resources. Diverse learning styles and preferences are catered to via interactive and personalized learning experiences offered by educational applications and platforms like Khan Academy, Coursera, and Duolingo.

The use of digital tools has completely changed how we approach professional growth and learning. Virtual classrooms, webinars, and online courses provide convenient and easily accessible ways to learn new things. A vast array of courses on many topics are available on e-learning platforms and frequently include interactive features like discussion boards, quizzes, and video lectures. Because of this flexibility, students may study according to their own timetable and speed, which makes education more accessible to people who lead busy lives or reside in remote places.

Digital technologies facilitate cooperative learning and information exchange as well. Connecting with classmates, teachers, and experts worldwide is made possible by online forums, social media, and collaborative tools. Through the promotion of a culture of ongoing learning and information sharing, this international network of educators and learners encourages people to interact with a variety of viewpoints and concepts. Digital technologies also make project-based learning and collaborative research easier, enabling teams to collaborate effectively no matter where they are physically located.

Higher education and professional training have seen especially significant transformations as a result of the use of digital tools in the classroom. With the help of online degree programs and certifications offered by universities and other organizations, students may obtain credentials from recognized universities without having to move. These courses provide students with a thorough and interesting education by including interactive assignments, virtual laboratories, and simulations. Individuals may remain up to date with the latest trends and breakthroughs in their areas by enrolling in industry-specific courses and training programs offered by professional development platforms like Udacity and LinkedIn Learning.

Digital tools and e-readers are beneficial for lifelong learning and personal enrichment. People may more easily pursue their interests and hobbies thanks to the accessibility and ease of digital books and internet resources. Digital tools offer a multitude of resources to promote intellectual curiosity and personal development, whether it be by reading classic literature, discovering new genres, or learning a new language. As an alternative to traditional reading, audiobooks—which can be accessed through services like Audible and Libby—allow people to enjoy books while multitasking, driving, or working out.

E-readers and other digital tools have many benefits, but there are drawbacks and restrictions to consider. The effect of digital reading on comprehension and retention is one of the main issues. Compared to reading paper books, some research indicates that reading on digital devices may result in worse comprehension and memory. Digital tools' interactive and multimedia capabilities can be both entertaining and distracting, which may lessen the depth of cognitive processing. Users should adopt efficient digital reading techniques, such as reducing distractions, taking notes, and actively interacting with the text, to allay these worries.

The problem of digital weariness and eye strain is another difficulty. Extended usage of digital screens can cause eye strain and discomfort, especially when reading on backlit tablets and smartphones. Although this problem is somewhat alleviated by e-readers using e-ink technology, consumers who use digital gadgets for prolonged periods of time should still be concerned. Users can take regular pauses, change the screen's settings, and adopt excellent ergonomics to reduce digital tiredness.

Another important factor to consider is digital accessibility. Not all digital information is equally accessible, even while e-readers and other digital technologies provide a wealth of accessibility capabilities. Digital books, websites, and applications can be made less usable for people with disabilities based on how they are designed and formatted. It is imperative that designers and developers give accessibility first priority when creating digital tools and resources so that everyone can use and benefit from them.

Another area of contention is the effect that digital gadgets like e-readers have on the environment. Although the manufacture of paper and physical books is lessened by digital reading, there is still an environmental cost associated with the creation, usage, and disposal of electronic gadgets. The extraction of raw materials, energy consumption, and the creation of electronic trash are all involved in the manufacture of e-readers and other digital gadgets. Customers may reduce these effects by using their gadgets responsibly, which includes prolonging their lifespan, recycling their electronic trash, and patronizing businesses that follow sustainable business practices.

Another issue affecting the uptake and effects of e-readers and other digital tools is the digital divide. There are significant regional and socioeconomic differences in access to digital gadgets and high-speed internet. Digital tools may make knowledge and education more accessible to all, yet unequal access can make inequality already present worse. For everyone to benefit from digital tools, efforts to close the digital divide—such as lowering the cost of devices, building up internet infrastructure, and giving instruction in digital literacy—are crucial.

There are concerns regarding data security and privacy when e-readers and digital technologies are used in educational and professional contexts. Personal data is frequently collected and stored when using digital platforms, which raises questions regarding how this data is handled and safeguarded. Users should be informed of privacy policies, and developers should put strong security mechanisms in place to protect user data. To foster confidence and safeguard user privacy, data practices must be held accountable and transparent.

Notwithstanding these difficulties, e-readers and digital technologies have enormous potential to improve learning, reading, and personal development. The power and influence of these instruments will grow as long as technology does. Digital reading and learning might become even more personalized and enhanced with the help of innovations like augmented reality, artificial intelligence, and adaptive learning algorithms.

E-readers and other digital tools can be significantly improved by artificial intelligence (AI). Recommendation engines driven by AI may make book and resource recommendations based on a user's reading tastes and history, assisting them in finding new material that interests them. In order to adapt instructional information to each person's unique learning style and speed, AI may also offer tailored learning routes and adaptive feedback. Artificial intelligence (AI)-powered language processing systems can also facilitate language acquisition, translation, and understanding, increasing the accessibility of digital information for a worldwide audience.

Innovative opportunities for interactive and immersive reading experiences are presented by augmented reality (AR). With AR technology, a mixed reading experience may be created by superimposing digital content over the real world. AR, for instance, can make tales come to life by animating scenes and characters and offering interactive features that captivate readers in fresh and interesting ways. With interactive diagrams, simulations, and visualizations, augmented reality (AR) may improve textbooks and learning materials in educational situations by increasing the accessibility and engagement of complicated subjects.

Digital learning aids may be improved even further by adaptive learning algorithms, which tailor instructional content based on data and analytics. These algorithms can evaluate a user's performance, pinpoint their advantages and disadvantages, and modify the information as necessary. By offering individualized resources and assistance that are tailored to the requirements of each individual, this personalized approach can enhance learning results. Moreover, mastery-based learning—in which students advance at their own speed and gain a better comprehension of the subject matter—can be aided by adaptive learning.

Improvements in connectivity and integration will also be seen in the future of digital tools and e-readers. The smooth integration of e-readers and digital tools with other digital systems and platforms will be made possible by the widespread use of smart technology and Internet of Things (IoT) devices. For instance, e-readers and smart home systems may sync to offer a synchronized reading experience across several devices. Smart glasses and fitness trackers are examples of wearable technology that may be integrated with digital tools to provide new methods of interacting with and consuming digital material.

Another development that will influence e-readers and digital tools in the future is the growth of digital libraries and open-access materials. A worldwide audience may access enormous volumes of books, research papers, and multimedia resources through digital libraries. Open-access projects facilitate the democratization of information by granting unlimited and free access to scientific publications. These initiatives also offer vital resources to scholars, students, and the general public. The proliferation of open-access resources and digital libraries will facilitate lifelong learning and increase the amount of knowledge available.

To sum up, e-readers and other digital tools have revolutionized the way we read, learn, and access information by providing a level of ease, flexibility, and accessibility never before possible. E-readers offer a convenient and portable reading experience thanks to their e-ink technology and customizable features. Digital technologies promote collaborative learning and information sharing. Examples of these tools are tablets, cell phones, and educational applications. With the help of these technological advancements, education, career advancement, and personal enrichment have all undergone radical change, making learning more interesting and accessible than ever.

Audiobooks and Their Role in Speed Reading

The introduction of technology has fundamentally changed the way we consume entertainment and information. The rise in popularity of audiobooks in this digital age is one noteworthy phenomenon. Audiobooks have completely changed how individuals read and consume information by providing a substitute for more conventional reading techniques. They are especially well-liked by people who want to improve their speed- reading skills. This section investigates the use of audiobooks for fast reading, looking at their advantages, disadvantages, and effects on comprehension and literacy.

With the help of audiobooks, readers may interact with literature in a novel way while completing other duties. One of the main factors contributing to the popularity of audiobooks is their ability to multitask. Audiobooks provide a useful option for people with hectic schedules, allowing them to "read" while driving, working out, or doing housework. Audiobooks are an excellent resource for anyone who wants to improve their reading speed and general productivity only because of their convenience.

The capacity of audiobooks to improve speed reading through aural stimulation is one of their main benefits. Skimming the text, utilizing peripheral vision, and reducing subvocalization—the internal voice that happens when reading silently—are common practices in traditional speed-reading methods. Conversely, audiobooks do not require visual processing or subvocalization at all. People who are listening to a narration can learn the material at a rate that may be challenging to do when reading silently. By assisting listeners in maintaining a steady reading pace, this auditory method can lower the chance of regression and enhance understanding in general.

Additionally, audiobooks' several playing choices might help you read faster. Users of most audiobook systems may change the playing speed to listen to books quicker without compromising understanding. Because it lets users progressively raise their listening pace over time, this function is very helpful for people who are practicing speed reading. People may train their brains to comprehend information more rapidly by gradually increasing the playback speed, which will ultimately improve their reading efficiency.

Audiobooks can help with understanding and information retention in addition to increasing speed reading. Studies have indicated that the cognitive processes involved in listening to audiobooks differ from those in regular reading. The brain analyzes auditory information when reading a book, which can boost memory retention by activating several neural pathways. By integrating visual and aural processing, this multimodal interaction might provide a greater comprehension of the subject matter. Professional narrators may also improve understanding by adding voice inflections, emotional subtleties, and emphasis on key themes that can be overlooked when reading silently.

For those who struggle with reading or vision issues, using audiobooks for fast reading has several advantages. For example, traditional reading can be a long and difficult process for those with dyslexia. As an accessible substitute, audiobooks let individuals appreciate reading without being limited by their condition. In a similar vein, those who are blind or visually impaired can benefit from audiobooks' aural format, which allows them to interact with written information without the need for Braille or other assistive devices. Audiobooks can encourage a love of reading and learning in those who might otherwise find it difficult to learn through traditional ways by making literature more accessible.

Notwithstanding the many benefits of audiobooks, it is imperative to contemplate possible demerits and constraints. One thing to keep in mind is that not every content is appropriate for audiobooks. They work well for fiction, biographies, and other narrative-driven genres, but they might not work as well for lengthy academic books or items that call for close reading, thoughtful consideration, and taking notes. Since audiobooks are linear, it may not be easy to go over particular passages again or cross-reference material, which is frequently required for professional or academic study. Additionally, publications that mainly rely on charts, drawings, or diagrams may find it disadvantageous because audiobooks lack these visual components.

The dependence of audiobooks on technology and the related expenses provide another possible disadvantage. Usually, you need a digital device and an audiobook service membership in order to access audiobooks. Although many public libraries provide free audiobook access, the selection of titles may be more restricted than with subscription services. Furthermore, some people may find the expense of buying audiobooks to be exorbitant, especially those who read a lot of books. This cost barrier could prevent audiobooks from becoming widely used as the main reading mode.

Another thing to worry about is how audiobooks will affect conventional reading practices. Some detractors contend that conventional reading abilities may deteriorate as a result of audiobooks' convenience. For instance, listening to audiobooks on a daily basis may cut down on the amount of time spent practicing silent reading, which may erode the ability to read deeply and analytically. Furthermore, compared to actively reading a physical or digital book, listening to an audiobook passively may make readers less interested since they may be more susceptible to distractions.

These worries must be weighed against the possible advantages of audiobooks in fostering a literacy and reading culture. People who do not normally read books can be introduced to literature through audiobooks. Audiobooks can encourage more people to read by making it easier and more convenient, allowing them to discover a wider range of genres, authors, and themes. A lifelong love of reading and learning may be fostered by this greater exposure to literature, which will ultimately lead to improved literacy rates and a better-informed public.

Additionally, the use of audiobooks in educational environments has demonstrated encouraging outcomes. Teachers are seeing more and more the benefits of audiobooks as an additional resource to enhance traditional reading instruction. When learning a language, audiobooks may be very helpful since they assist pupils in becoming more proficient in listening and pronouncing words correctly. They can also offer a welcoming and inclusive learning environment for children with different requirements, guaranteeing that all students, irrespective of reading level, have access to the same material.

Audiobooks play a significant part in lifelong learning and professional growth in addition to rapid reading. In the fast-paced world of today, ongoing education is crucial for both personal and professional development. For working individuals who wish to keep current on industry advancements, audiobooks provide a useful option. People who listen to audiobooks on their commute or while working out can make better use of their time and learn important information. This strategy may develop a culture of continuous improvement, increase productivity, and improve professional abilities.

Furthermore, the distinction between conventional reading and listening has become increasingly hazy with the growth of podcasts and other audio material. A vast array of subjects is covered by numerous podcasts, ranging from literature and history to science and technology. People may now easily absorb information and stay informed because of this trend's seamless integration of audio material into daily activities. The rising acceptance of auditory learning as a valid and efficient way to learn is demonstrated by the popularity of audiobooks and podcasts.

To sum up, audiobooks have become an effective tool for raising literacy levels and improving the speed of reading in the digital age. People with hectic schedules, vision impairments, or reading difficulties frequently choose them because of their capacity to offer an easy and accessible reading experience. Audiobooks provide enhanced reading speed, comprehension, and information retention through a range of playing choices and cognitive stimulation. Notwithstanding certain disadvantages like access fees and content restrictions, audiobooks have a big impact on encouraging a love of reading and promoting lifelong learning. The use of audiobooks in education and fast reading is anticipated to grow as technology develops, drastically changing the way people interact with information and literature.

Professional Applications: Meetings, Emails, and Reports

Meetings, emails, and reports are essential components of teamwork and communication in the context of professional applications. These technologies make it easier to coordinate tasks, share information, and make decisions—all of which are crucial for accomplishing corporate objectives. It is essential to comprehend the subtleties of these communication techniques and apply them skillfully if you want to increase output, promote a happy workplace, and achieve success. This section explores the importance, best practices, and difficulties of using meetings, emails, and reports professionally in today's workplace.

Meetings are essential for organizational communication because they provide a forum for idea sharing, problem resolution, and strategic decision-making. They can be held in a variety of settings, such as official board meetings, relaxed team gatherings, and online conferences. Bringing stakeholders together to share information, give updates, and work together on projects is the main goal of every meeting. Clear agendas, well-defined goals, and engaged attendance are hallmarks of effective meetings. An agenda acts as a guide, listing the subjects to be covered and guaranteeing that the meeting remains on topic and fruitful. It is essential to distribute the agenda in advance so that attendees may get ready and participate fully in the conversations.

An essential component of running a productive meeting is preparation. Prior to participating, participants should read pertinent resources, compile the information they'll need, and prepare their ideas. This proactive attitude shows respect for other people's time and work, and it also improves the quality of talks. The chairman or facilitator is essential in directing the discussion, making sure everyone is heard, and striking a balance between opposing points of view throughout the meeting. Establishing a collaborative environment and reaching a consensus requires open communication, constructive criticism, and active listening.

Due to technological improvements and the growing trend of remote work, virtual meetings have become more and more common in today's digital era. Flexible scheduling, financial savings, and the opportunity to interact with participants across large distances are just a few advantages of virtual meetings. They do, however, also bring special difficulties, such as time zone variations, technological problems, and the possibility of lower involvement. Selecting trustworthy communication channels, establishing explicit guidelines for online contacts, and promoting active engagement with interactive elements, visual assistance, and frequent check-ins are crucial steps in reducing these difficulties.

Meetings are essential for organizational communication, but in order to prevent meeting overload, they must be handled carefully. Employee dissatisfaction, exhaustion, and lower productivity can result from too many meetings. It is critical to assess the need for each meeting and determine whether the goals may be accomplished via email or other collaboration technologies. Organizations may make the most use of their time and resources by giving high-impact meetings a priority and organizing the meeting agenda in an efficient manner.

Another essential element of business communication is email, which is a flexible tool for information sharing, task coordination, and record keeping. They are frequently utilized for many different things, such as client contacts, corporate communication, and formal letters. Email efficacy depends on their professionalism, clarity, and conciseness. A well-written email should contain a subject line that is obvious, a message that is brief and pertinent, and a tone that is kind and respectful. Email receivers should be able to prioritize and reply appropriately if the subject line adequately summarizes the content of the message. The email's body should be rationally organized, with the main ideas being emphasized and any necessary supporting information included. Implementing numbered lists or bullet points can improve reading and make comprehension easier.

Email correspondence must always be professional, as it represents the sender's authority and the reputation of the company. To come out as polished and professional, use proper language, punctuation, and spelling. Furthermore, it's critical to utilize proper salutations, titles, and signatures based on the situation and the recipient's connection. To start, a professional email to a client or senior executive should say "Dear [Name]," and it should end with a formal ending like "Sincerely" or "Best regards," which should be followed by the sender's name and contact details.

Emails' capacity to provide asynchronous communication, enabling receivers to reply whenever it's most convenient for them, is one of its main benefits. When working in international companies with team members in various time zones, flexibility is very beneficial. But if they're not handled well, emails' asynchronous nature can also cause delays and miscommunications. To ensure rapid replies and prevent confusion, clear and concise communication is essential. It's critical to respond to emails immediately, give updates on unfinished business, and acknowledge receipt of any questions or concerns.

Emails are a useful tool for record-keeping and documentation as well. They offer a written record of talks, choices, and agreements that may be referred to at a later time if necessary. This is especially crucial in administrative, financial, and legal settings where proper documentation is necessary for responsibility and compliance. To manage the email inbox effectively and access information quickly when needed, folder-based organization of emails, the use of filters and tags, and the preservation of significant communication are all recommended.

Emails have many advantages, but there are drawbacks as well. Every day, emails might be excessive in quantity, which can cause information overload and lower productivity. Effective email inbox management calls for planning, organization, and strategic prioritizing. Some strategies to lessen these difficulties include scheduling dedicated periods of time to review emails, unsubscribing from pointless mailing lists, and employing filters to prioritize and classify communications. Remembering proper email etiquette also means avoiding abusing "Reply All," communicating in a clear and pertinent manner, and, unless absolutely required, not sending emails after regular business hours.

Another essential component of professional communication is the report, which acts as a formal channel for information, analysis, and advice. They are used to record research findings, project progress, financial performance, and strategic goals in a variety of settings, including industry, academia, and government. Standardized elements such as the title page, executive summary, introduction, methodology, findings, analysis, conclusions, and recommendations are often included in reports. Clarity, accuracy, and coherence are always crucial, but a report's form and content might change based on its audience and goal.

An executive summary, which offers a succinct synopsis of the key ideas and conclusions, is an essential part of a report. It should be written in a clear, concise manner so that readers can understand the main points of the report without becoming bogged down in the specifics. The backdrop is established in the introduction, which also describes the goals, parameters, and importance of the report. In addition to giving background information, it should describe the important terminology and ideas that the report uses.

The steps and methods used to collect and examine the data are described in depth in the methodology section. In order to enable readers to comprehend the foundation of the results and evaluate their validity, it should be thorough and straightforward. The data is presented, and the results are interpreted, emphasizing trends, patterns, and insights in the findings and analysis sections. Tables, charts, and graphs are examples of visual aids that may improve data presentation and make comprehension easier. The findings are summarized in the conclusions and suggestions section, which also provides practical advice based on the analysis and logical conclusions. It should serve as a road map for upcoming decisions or activities and be precise, achievable, and unambiguous.

A report's quality is dependent on its critical analysis, extensive research, and lucid language. Using trustworthy and reputable sources, properly citing references, and presenting facts honestly are all crucial. To guarantee a polished and professional report, further requirements include correct formatting, uniformity in style and tone, and attention to detail. Editing and proofreading are essential phases in the report-writing process because they make it possible to find and fix mistakes, contradictions, and ambiguities.

In professional contexts, reports have a variety of uses, from directing decision-making and providing information to documenting progress and guaranteeing responsibility. They play a crucial role in project management, performance assessment, and strategic planning. Project reports, on the other hand, track the progress of initiatives, identify challenges, and suggest solutions to ensure that projects stay on track and meet their objectives. Financial reports, for example, offer insights into an organization's financial health, enabling informed decisions on budgeting, investments, and resource allocation. Research reports assist innovation and evidence-based practices by generating and disseminating information.

Report writing may be difficult and time-consuming work, even with its importance. Proficiency in the subject topic and a blend of analytical, writing, and organizing abilities are essential. It's critical to begin the report-writing process with a clear plan, collect pertinent data in an organized manner, and stay in constant contact with stakeholders in order to simplify the process. Software and collaborative tools can help with cooperation by enabling several participants to work on various report portions at the same time. Templates and style guides may also guarantee adherence to corporate standards and offer a uniform foundation.

To sum up, emails, reports, and meetings are essential instruments for professional communication. They all play different but complementary functions in promoting communication, teamwork, and decision-making. Careful preparation, engaged participation, and a focus on specific goals and outcomes are necessary for meetings to be effective. Emails are a versatile and effective communication tool that allows for information documentation and asynchronous conversations. Reports help responsible decision-making by offering an organized and formal means of presenting facts, analysis, and recommendations. In today's dynamic and connected world, professionals who want to improve productivity, encourage teamwork, and achieve organizational success must become proficient in these communication techniques. Organizations may enhance their communication strategy and foster continuous development by utilizing best practices, resolving obstacles, and adopting new technologies.

CHAPTER V

Long-Term Maintenance and Improvement

Continuing Practice and Refinement

To achieve mastery in any subject, one must have dedication, tenacity, and a commitment to continuously practicing and improving their skills. The pursuit of greatness is a never-ending process that involves studying, practicing, and perfecting one's skills. This is true whether one is pursuing excellence in the arts, sciences, sports, or professions. The purpose of this section is to investigate the significance of continuous practice and refining in the process of attaining mastery, as well as the principles that direct this process and the influence it has on both personal and professional growth.

A fundamental understanding that mastery is not a fixed state but rather a journey that is ongoing is the foundation upon which the concept of continuous practice and refining is built. In order to achieve excellence in any endeavor, one must have a strong dedication to the process of continual development. Throughout this journey, careful practice, feedback, and a willingness to push oneself beyond one's comfort zone are all essential components. Efforts that are concentrated and directed toward the improvement of particular components of performance are what constitute deliberate practice. The process is defined by the establishment of distinct objectives, the division of difficult tasks into components that are more achievable, and the methodical attention paid to areas that require enhancement. The purpose of this kind of exercise is not to engage in mindless repetition but rather to participate in activities that test one's existing capabilities and foster physical and mental development.

Within the context of the process of continuous practice and improvement, feedback is an extremely important component. The provision of constructive feedback offers individuals vital insights into their areas of strength and areas in which they can improve, so leading them on their journey toward mastery. The process of soliciting input from mentors, peers, and experts results in a more comprehensive perspective and assists in the identification of blind spots. When receiving feedback, it is critical to approach it with an open mind and a willingness to learn. The cultivation of a growth mindset, which is essential for continual improvement, can be accomplished by viewing feedback not as criticism but as an opportunity for personal development. Carol Dweck, a psychologist, is the one who came up with the term "growth mindset," which refers to the concept that one's capabilities and intelligence can be improved by the application of work, learning, and perseverance. Individuals who adopt this mentality are more likely to regard obstacles as chances for personal development and to persevere in the face of failures.

The notion of incremental progress is another factor that plays a role in the process of continuous practice and improvement. To gain mastery, one must make incremental, continuous improvements over the course of time. Individuals should concentrate on making consistent improvements in their knowledge and abilities rather than trying to bring about significant changes in their lives. The Japanese idea of "kaizen," which translates to "continuous improvement," is a strategy that is consistent with this approach. The concept of Kaizen places an emphasis on the significance of making smaller, more gradual adjustments that, when taken together, result in considerable advancements. Individuals have the potential to achieve significant improvement over the course of a lengthy period of time if they make it a daily goal to improve, even if it is only by a small margin.

To continue practicing and improving one's skills, it is impossible to exaggerate the need for discipline and tenacity. If one wishes to achieve mastery, one must possess a high level of dedication and the ability to remain devoted to their goals in spite of obstacles and failures. Maintaining a consistent practice schedule, allocating time for concentrated work, and guarding against the temptation to take shortcuts are all essential components of practicing discipline. On the other hand, perseverance may be defined as the capacity to persevere in the face of challenges and to continue moving forward even when it appears that progress is being made at a steady pace. As a result of the fact that the path to mastery is frequently lengthy and challenging, the capacity to maintain one's motivation and resilience is essential to overcoming challenges and attaining achievement.

One of the most important components of ongoing practice and improvement is the significance of establishing goals that are SMART, which stands for specific, measurable, attainable, relevant, and time-bound. Individuals are able to maintain their concentration and motivation with the assistance of SMART goals, which offer a clear framework for success. Having a clear grasp of what has to be accomplished is made possible via the setting of explicit goals, while individuals are able to measure their progress through the completion of measurable goals. Achievable goals ensure that the targets that are set are reasonable and attainable, relevant goals match with one's long-term aspirations, and time-bound goals create a sense of urgency and a deadline for the fulfillment of the goals. Individuals have the ability to develop a road map for their path toward mastery and successfully monitor their progress once they have established SMART goals for themselves.

In addition to being a process limited to individual endeavors, continuous practice, and refining also extends to situations involving organizations and teams. When it comes to the business world, organizations that place a high priority on learning and continuous development are in a better position to adjust to shifting surroundings and achieve sustained success. Taking this strategy, which is frequently referred to as a learning company, places an emphasis on the significance of cultivating a culture that values ongoing education and skill development. Employees are encouraged to seek out new knowledge, share their thoughts, and collaborate on innovative solutions when working for a business that places a strong emphasis on learning. Through the implementation of this culture of continuous improvement, the performance of the company is driven, and the overall efficacy of the team is improved.

Innovation is yet another essential component of ongoing practice and improvement responsibilities. By pushing the limits of what is possible and exploring new ways of thinking and doing, the quest for mastery frequently requires pushing the boundaries of what is possible. To innovate, one must be willing to explore, willing to take chances, and willing to learn from mistakes. A culture of innovation allows individuals and organizations to stay ahead of the curve and continuously enhance their processes, products, and services. This can be accomplished by cultivating an innovative culture. Because of the quick pace of change in today's world, where technical developments and global trends are continually reshaping sectors and marketplaces, the capacity to innovate and adapt is of utmost importance.

Additionally, the significance of mentoring and coaching in the process of ongoing practice and improvement must be considered. Individuals are able to traverse their road toward mastery with the assistance of mentors and coaches who provide them with advice, support, and useful insights. They provide a wealth of expertise and knowledge, assisting mentees in identifying areas in which they may improve, setting objectives that are attainable, and developing techniques that are beneficial for expanding their capabilities. Trust, respect, and a shared commitment to the well-being of the mentee are the foundations upon which the mentor-mentee relationship is constructed. Facilitating continual progress and assisting individuals in reaching their maximum potential are two of the most important roles that mentors and coaches perform. They do this by giving individuals with constructive feedback, encouragement, and accountability.

When it comes to ongoing practice and improvement, self-reflection is an essential component, in addition to receiving support from outside sources. The act of frequently evaluating one's performance, determining one's strengths and limitations, and making modifications as required is what is meant by the term "self-reflection." Through the process of reflection, individuals get a more profound comprehension of their progress as well as the areas in which they might improve. Some of the tools that can help foster self-reflection include keeping a journal, practicing meditation, and engaging in mindfulness activities. Individuals are able to cultivate a deeper sense of self-awareness and make decisions regarding their practice and development that are more informed when they take the time to reflect on their experiences and learn from them.

Continuous practice and improvement have a significant impact on both one's personal and professional development through their impact. On a more personal level, the dedication to continual development helps to cultivate a sense of purpose, fulfillment, and self-efficacy. People are inspired to follow their interests, triumph over obstacles, and accomplish their objectives as a result of this incentive. The process of achieving mastery also fosters personal development, resiliency, and flexibility, all of which are key attributes for successfully navigating the complexities and uncertainties of life.

On a professional level, continuous practice and refining leads to improvements in job performance, career progression, and the efficacy of leadership. When it comes to maintaining their relevance in their respective professions, adapting to new technologies and trends, and producing high-quality work, professionals who are committed to continual learning and improvement are better equipped. They differentiate themselves from their contemporaries and provide possibilities for professional development and advancement as a result of their dedication to quality. In addition, leaders who place a priority on continuous improvement serve as models for their teams, which in turn inspires a culture of excellence and propels the success of the organization.

It is equally important to note that the pursuit of continuous practice and improvement has wider-ranging ramifications for society. The dedication to continuous improvement has a direct impact on the quality of services and goods that are offered to the general public in disciplines such as medicine, education, and engineering. As an illustration, medical practitioners who participate in continual education and training are better suited to provide high-quality patient care and to remain current with the most recent breakthroughs in their industry. In a similar vein, in order to build more effective learning environments and better promote student accomplishment, educators who consistently modify their teaching approaches and remain updated about educational research can effectively construct these environments.

When it comes to the world of sports, the concept of continuous practice and improvement is demonstrated by athletes who devote endless hours to training and perfecting their specialized abilities. Acquiring a combination of physical conditioning, technical expertise, and mental fortitude is necessary in order to achieve excellence in sports. There is a greater likelihood that athletes will achieve success and realize their full potential if they engage in purposeful practice, seek feedback from coaches, and continually strive to improve their performance. As they make their way toward mastery, the principles of discipline, patience, and gradual development are essential components of their path.

When it comes to the arts, it is vital to engage in continuous practice and refinement in order to cultivate creativity, technical skills, and artistic expression. Artists, musicians, authors, and performers all engage in consistent practice, experimentation, and introspection in order to hone their profession and produce work of superior quality. They are able to push the limits of their creativity, experiment with new methods and styles, and establish a more profound connection with their audience as a result of their dedication to constant growth. An unwavering commitment to learning, development, and self-expression over one's entire life is a defining characteristic of the path to artistic mastery.

In conclusion, pursuing mastery in various subjects and disciplines requires a commitment to ongoing practice and refining as core principles. To achieve excellence, one must engage in a continuous process that includes focused practice, feedback, incremental growth, and self-reflection. Individuals are able to overcome obstacles and accomplish their objectives when they possess fundamental qualities such as discipline, tenacity, and a growth mentality. These attributes are the driving force behind continuous improvement. The influence of continuous practice and improvement extends beyond the realm of human growth, as it has the potential to affect not just professional achievement but also organizational performance and the general well-being of society.

Through the adoption of these principles, individuals and organizations have the ability to cultivate a culture that values excellence, creativity, and continuous learning, ultimately leading to the realization of their full potential and making a positive contribution to the world.

Common Challenges and How to Address Them

The capacity to read quickly is a vital skill that gives various benefits, including the ability to take in huge amounts of information in a short amount of time, enhanced productivity, and improved comprehension. Being able to perfect speed reading, on the other hand, might be difficult due to the many difficulties that individuals face along the route. One of the goals of this section is to ensure that readers are able to make the most of their potential and improve their reading experience by examining the common problems that are encountered during speed reading and providing techniques to overcome those challenges effectively.

Subvocalization, which is the practice of secretly pronouncing words in one's thoughts while reading, is one of the most common problems that people face when trying to improve their reading speed. When reading, the speed of reading is substantially slowed down by subvocalization since it restricts the tempo to the speed of speech. Subvocalization can be reduced or eliminated entirely by the practice of techniques that readers can use to solve this issue. Utilizing a pacer, such as a finger or a pen, to direct the eyes along the lines of text is one way that has proven to be effective. It is through this physical action that the eyes are encouraged to move more quickly, which in turn lessens the tendency to subvocalize. In addition, readers can give themselvesthe opportunity to practice reading chunks of words or phrases rather than individual words, which will educate their brains to detect and process groups of words concurrently.

The practice of regression, which is the habit of rereading or going back to literature that has already been read, is another typical obstacle in the way of speed reading. The flow of reading is disrupted by regression, which also contributes to a decrease in overall speed and understanding. To be successful in overcoming this obstacle, readers should concentrate on refining their ability to concentrate and minimizing distractions. It is possible to improve concentration and reduce the need for regression by establishing an atmosphere that is conducive to reading by removing acoustic distractions and interruptions. In addition, the utilization of a pacemaker can assist in the preservation of forward momentum and discourage the act of retracing. Reducing the temptation to retreat and improving attention are two additional benefits that can be gained from practicing mindfulness techniques such as meditation or deep breathing.

There are also considerable difficulties in the way of speed reading, such as poor eye movement and coordination. Inefficient eye movement patterns are common among readers. These patterns include fixating on each word individually or making unnecessary stops and hops in the reading process. Reading speed is slowed down and comprehension is hindered as a result of these patterns. Readers can enhance their visual tracking and coordination by engaging in eye training exercises, which can help them overcome this difficulty. Utilizing flashcards that include words or phrases and gradually increasing the speed at which they are given is an excellent practice that may be taken advantage of. In order to educate the eyes to move swiftly and smoothly across the text, this exercise is performed. One such method is to practice reading vertically, which involves scanning columns of text from top to bottom rather than from left to right. Through the use of this strategy, eye movement is encouraged to be more efficient, and unwanted stops and jumps are reduced.

Another essential component of fast reading is comprehension, which can be one of the most difficult aspects to retain at greater reading speeds. There is a widespread concern among readers that raising their reading pace will lead to a reduction in their comprehension and ability to remember the information. It is essential to find a middle ground between speed and comprehension in order to address this challenge. Previewing the content before reading it in great detail is a practice that has proven to be beneficial. To accomplish this, you will need to go through the headers, subheadings, and important points in order to gain an overall picture of the content. By doing so, readers are able to activate their existing knowledge and construct a conceptual framework for the material, which significantly improves their ability to comprehend and remember the information. Additionally, the use of active reading techniques, such as highlighting important information or taking brief notes, can strengthen comprehension and make it easier to recall important information.

One of the challenges that comes with fast reading is coping with content that could be more familiar or easier. Readers may struggle to maintain their speed and comprehension when confronted with materials that are dense or technical. When attempting to solve this problem, it is absolutely necessary to modify reading tactics according to the level of difficulty of the information. Readers have the option of employing a strategy known as selective reading when it comes to content that is less familiar or technical. To accomplish this, it is necessary to determine which parts of the text are the most important and to concentrate on those areas while skimming over the parts that are less important. Readers can keep their pace without sacrificing their ability to comprehend the material if they prioritize the most important information. In addition, preventing cognitive overload and improving general comprehension can be accomplished by breaking down difficult material into smaller, more digestible chunks and taking rests in between each of these chunks.

When it comes to improving skills in speed reading, one of the most prevalent challenges is a need for more practice and consistency. The ability to read quickly takes consistent practice and devotion, just like any other skill, in order to become proficient. Although they begin with a lot of excitement, many readers need help to stick to a continuous practice program. The establishment of a disciplined practice regimen and the setting of precise goals are both essential in order to be successful in overcoming this obstacle. Even if it is only for a few minutes, having a certain amount of time set aside each day for the purpose of practicing speed reading can result in substantial progress over the course of time. Keeping practice sessions interesting and varied can also be accomplished by utilizing a wide range of reading resources, such as books, articles, and stuff hosted on the internet. In order to offer motivation and reinforce the habit of regular practice, it is helpful to keep track of progress and to celebrate even the smallest of accomplishments along the road.

The worry of missing out on crucial information is one of the psychological hurdles that a person has when trying to read fast. Readers may be concerned that if they read too rapidly, they will fail to get the complete meaning of the text or end up missing important elements. Fear like this can lead to anxiety, which in turn can impede the development of skills related to fast reading. In order to address this worry, it is essential to develop self-assurance and trust in one's capacity to absorb information at a faster rate. When beginning, it is helpful to practice with material that is familiar and less critical. This can assist in building confidence, which can then be transitioned to more significant literature. A further benefit of utilizing tactics such as summarizing key points or discussing the subject with others is that it can help to reinforce understanding and provide reassurance that essential information is not being overlooked.

When it comes to speed reading, one of the challenges that one faces is the task of balancing diverse levels of difficulty and readability across different texts. Certain books are plain and simple to read in a short amount of time, while others are more complicated and demand a longer pace of reading. In order to overcome this obstacle, readers need to cultivate the ability to modify their reading speed in accordance with the level of difficulty of the information they are reading. Recognizing when to slow down for more difficult parts and when to speed up for easier parts is a necessary step in this process. It is possible to determine the level of complexity of the material by employing strategies such as scanning and skimming and then modifying the pace of the reading accordingly. Through the cultivation of this flexibility, readers are able to maintain an optimal balance between speed and understanding across a variety of text formats.

When reading, the usage of digital devices and displays brings its own unique set of problems, which might make fast reading more difficult. Reading on displays, such as those seen on computers, tablets, or smartphones, can cause eye strain and have an impact on both the pace and comprehension of information being read. There is a pressing need to improve the quality of the digital reading experience to solve this matter. Eye strain can be alleviated and readability can be improved by adjusting the brightness of the screen, using appropriate text sizes, and eliminating glare. In addition, the utilization of digital tools and applications that are constructed particularly for speed reading can improve the overall reading experience. These applications typically include functions that allow for the adjustment of reading speeds, the marking of progress, and the tracking of progress, all of which can facilitate the practice of speed reading and improve efficiency.

In addition, one of the challenges associated with fast reading is preventing burnout and retaining enthusiasm. The process of acquiring skills in fast reading can be challenging and requires consistent work because of its demanding nature. At the same time, it is essential to maintain one's motivation and discover ways to make the practice pleasurable and enjoyable. It is possible to have a sense of accomplishment and be motivated by setting milestones that are within one's reach and rewarding oneself for completing those milestones. It is possible to keep the practice sessions interesting and minimize monotony by exploring a variety of reading materials and themes that are of interest to the individual. It is possible to receive support, motivation, and a sense of accountability by participating in online communities or joining speed reading groups. In order for readers to maintain their dedication to speed reading and continue to make progress, it is important for them to maintain their motivation and find joy in the process.

Lastly, one of the most significant obstacles that must be overcome in order to achieve fast reading is the requirement for individualized approaches and strategies. Each individual reader is one of a kind, with their own set of preferences, strengths, and characteristics. One person's solution might not be applicable to another's situation. It is essential to try out a variety of methods and approaches in order to determine which one would be most suitable for one's specific requirements and objectives. In order to accomplish this, it may be necessary to experiment with various techniques for lowering subvocalization, to try out eye training exercises, or to modify reading tactics according to the sort of material being read. It is possible to gain useful insights and assist in the development of a personalized strategy for speed reading by keeping a notebook or record of practice sessions, noting what works and what does not provide the desired results.

Taking on the common obstacles that are associated with speed reading calls for a combination of methods and techniques that are adapted to the specific requirements of each individual. Readers are able to overcome challenges and improve their speed-reading abilities by limiting the amount of subvocalization they engage in, minimizing regression, enhancing eye movement and coordination, retaining comprehension, and adapting to different levels of difficulty. For ongoing improvement and advancement, it is necessary to engage in regular practice, receive feedback, and engage in self-reflection. In addition, the development of speed-reading skills can be further supported by optimizing the digital reading experience, keeping motivation under control, and adopting tailored techniques. Individuals are able to unleash the full potential of speed reading and reap its multiple benefits in both their personal and professional undertakings if they are dedicated, persistent, and employ the appropriate tactics.

Joining Speed Reading Groups or Workshops

Acquiring the talent of speed reading holds the alluring possibility of rapidly and effectively processing vast quantities of information. Gaining proficiency in this talent may benefit many people by increasing their output, academic achievement, and professional abilities. While internet tools and solo practice may help in the quest to become a skilled speed reader, participating in speed reading workshops or groups provides a controlled, supportive, and engaging atmosphere that can greatly accelerate the learning process. This section examines the advantages of taking part in workshops or speed- reading groups, the dynamics of these learning settings, and how these factors affect the growth of speed-reading abilities.

The controlled learning environment that speed reading clubs and seminars offer is one of the main benefits of attending them. In contrast to self-study, which is sometimes erratic and disorganized, groups and workshops are usually conducted by knowledgeable teachers who walk participants through a well-planned curriculum. With this methodical approach, students are certain to master every facet of speed reading, from basic skills to sophisticated tactics. Participants may ask questions, get rapid feedback, and get their worries cleared up when a skilled instructor is present. This helps speed up learning and helps participants avoid frequent traps.

Apart from the advantages of organized education, speed reading clubs and seminars provide an interactive and cooperative setting that encourages drive and responsibility. Learning in a group environment enables individuals to talk about their accomplishments, struggles, and experiences with others who share their objectives. This feeling of community fosters a welcoming environment where people may inspire and support one another, which can be immensely motivating. Additionally, the accountability that comes with belonging to a group helps motivate members to continue practicing and using the skills they acquire.

The ability to practice on real reading material under the guidance of professionals is another great benefit of speed-reading groups and seminars. In order to assist students to improve and hone their speed-reading abilities, instructors in these environments frequently employ a range of exercises and activities. These might consist of comprehension exams, eye movement exercises, and timed reading drills. When these methods are used in a controlled setting, participants may get quick feedback and change as necessary. Furthermore, teachers have the ability to present fresh and creative approaches that students would not come across during independent study, expanding their toolkit for fast reading techniques.

The use of gamification and competition in speed reading groups and seminars increases the learning experience through their participatory character. Friendly contests can improve learning engagement and enjoyment. Examples of these are comprehension challenges and reading races. In addition to being enjoyable, these activities motivate participants to challenge themselves and aim for better results. The use of gamification strategies, including awarding points or badges for accomplishments, can encourage individuals to practice frequently and monitor their improvement.

Additionally, seminars and speed-reading groups can give participants access to a multitude of tools that may not be easily accessible to individual students. Specialized reading materials, software, and tools for improving speed reading abilities are some examples of these resources. Teachers may also impart insightful advice, practical methods, and insights gleaned from their own experience and knowledge. Having access to these materials greatly enhances the educational process and provides participants with the resources they need to be successful.

The emphasis on understanding, in addition to speed, is one of the main features of speed-reading classes. Although the main objective is to increase reading speed, it's also critical to make sure that comprehension and retention are maintained. These courses' instructors usually stress how crucial it is to strike a balance between comprehension and speed. To improve understanding, they might present strategies like reading aloud, highlighting important details, and providing a summary of the content. Participants can create a more comprehensive reading strategy that enables them to absorb information rapidly without losing comprehension by emphasizing both speed and comprehension.

Speed reading classes and workshops can enhance not just reading comprehension and speed but also other cognitive abilities. For instance, a lot of speed-reading strategies incorporate workouts that strengthen eye coordination and movement, which helps increase visual processing skills. Furthermore, developing one's ability to recognize and comprehend important information swiftly might enhance analytical and critical thinking abilities. Participants can improve their general capacity for learning and problem-solving by honing these cognitive skills, which can be advantageous in both academic and professional contexts.

The social component of workshops and speed-reading groups is also essential to improving the educational process. Interacting with other participants offers a platform for networking, cooperation, and idea sharing.

Individuals can obtain fresh insights, forge new bonds with one another, and learn from one another's experiences. People who find learning fast reading to be lonely or tedious find this social connection to be especially beneficial. Working together to achieve a similar objective may develop enduring relationships and strengthen a feeling of community.

Workshops and speed-reading clubs can also offer a forum for discussing personal difficulties and roadblocks. Teachers can provide participants with individualized advice and assistance to help them get over any obstacles they may face. Tailored attention from a specialist may be helpful when it comes to subvocalization, boosting understanding, or increasing focus. In addition, the group environment enables members to talk about their struggles and get support and guidance from others who may have gone through comparable experiences. This collaborative approach to problem-solving can result in more confident and successful solutions.

In addition, speed reading workshops and groups frequently incorporate follow-up sessions and continuous coaching to make sure that learners keep improving even after the original instruction. These follow-up sessions can assist in strengthening the skills acquired, addressing any fresh difficulties that may emerge, and offering more encouragement to stick with the practice. Continual assistance from teachers and classmates may be very helpful in keeping the momentum continuing and guaranteeing long-term success in improving one's speed reading abilities.

Speed reading seminars and groups provide advantages for educational institutions and organizations in addition to the individual participants. To assist pupils in improving their reading and learning skills, speed reading workshops can be incorporated into the curricula of schools, colleges, and universities. Educational institutions may enhance academic achievement, cultivate a passion for reading, and better prepare students for future problems by teaching them how to read quickly. In a similar vein, companies might include training on rapid reading in their professional development initiatives. Workers who are fast readers and processors of information are better able to manage the responsibilities of their jobs, make wise judgments, and maintain their competitiveness.

Even while participating in speed reading groups and workshops has many benefits, there are some possible drawbacks that should be considered, along with solutions. A prevalent obstacle is the disparity in skill levels among the players. People may learn at various rates and from different beginning places in a group environment, which can make it challenging for teachers to meet everyone's requirements. Teachers can address this problem by using differentiated teaching strategies, which involve assigning assignments and giving feedback based on the proficiency level of each student. Additionally, participants may be guaranteed to receive the right amount of challenge and assistance by dividing individuals into smaller subgroups according to competence levels.

The possibility of information overload is another difficulty. Some participants may need help with speed reading courses since they cover a lot of material in a short amount of time. Teachers can address this by emphasizing skill development gradually, teaching new approaches step-by-step, and providing ample opportunity for practice and reinforcement. Preventing cognitive overload and ensuring more effective learning may be achieved by encouraging participants to concentrate on mastering one skill at a time before moving on to the next.

For some people, attending speed reading seminars might be too expensive. Although it may be beneficial to spend on high-quality training and materials, it's crucial to make sure that a wide range of participants can attend the workshops. Workshops can be made more inexpensive by providing payment plans, sliding scale pricing, or grants. Moreover, companies and academic institutions that understand the long-term advantages of improved reading abilities might pay for their staff members' or students' training.

Participating in speed reading workshops or groups has several advantages that may greatly improve learning and the advancement of speed-reading abilities. The best conditions for learning speed reading strategies are provided by an organized learning environment, professional coaching, practical experience, and a friendly atmosphere. The learning process is further enhanced by the focus on understanding, social engagement, and the development of cognitive skills. Speed reading groups and workshops may give people, companies, and educational institutions great chances to meet their reading objectives and realize their full potential by addressing any obstacles and guaranteeingaccessibility. A significant step in becoming a more proficient and successful reader is taking part in speed reading groups or workshops, whether for academic achievement, professional growth, or personal enrichment.

Staying Updated with New Techniques and Research

One of the most useful skills in today's fast-paced environment, when information overload is a typical difficulty, is the ability to read something quickly. Individuals who possess this ability are able to process and comprehend vast amounts of text in a quick and effective manner. On the other hand, just like any other ability, speed reading techniques are constantly evolving, and it is vital to stay current with new approaches and research in order to get the most of the benefits. Within the scope of this section, the significance of speed reading, the development of its methods, the function of technology, and the means by which one can remain current with the most recent research and practices in the field are discussed.

There is no possible way to overestimate the impact of fast reading. The capacity to swiftly assimilate and comprehend knowledge can contribute to increased productivity and success in a variety of circumstances, including academic settings, professional settings, and personal settings. The ability to read quickly can help pupils improve their academic performance and study more effectively. For professionals, this can mean staying ahead of the competition in a job market that is very competitive by remaining current with the latest advancements and trends in their industry. On a more personal level, fast reading can improve one's ability to study throughout their entire life and broaden their knowledge base.

The urge to break old reading habits that limit reading speed and comprehension is the driving force behind the development of approaches intended to speed up the reading process. The practice of subvocalization, in which readers silently utter words in their minds, is frequently encountered in traditional reading scenarios. Because it relates the speed of reading to the speed of speech, this practice makes reading more difficult. In the beginning, the strategies for speed reading concentrated on lowering the amount of subvocalization and expanding the span of recognition. This allowed readers to digest larger sections of text rather than individual words. Methods such as the practice of reading groups of words rather than single words and the use of a pacer (a finger or pen) to guide the eyes were among the first strategies developed to improve reading speed. Other methods included the practice of reading single words first.

Over time, new methods came into being, which were influenced by developments in cognitive psychology and neuroscience. A method that falls into this category is called meta-guiding, and it involves the utilization of visual aids in order to train the eyes to go smoothly and quickly across the page. Regressions, in which the eyes move backward to reread the text, are reduced with the use of this strategy, which helps lessen fixations. An additional method is peripheral vision training, which involves expanding the reader's range of vision in order to take in a greater number of words immediately. This strategy makes use of the brain's capacity to process information in a peripheral manner, which results in an increase in reading speed without affecting understanding.

Because of the introduction of new tools and resources, the advent of technology has brought about a revolution in the field of fast reading. Personalized training programs are available through software apps and online platforms. These programs are designed to adjust to the user's reading habits and progress. The eye-tracking technology that is frequently incorporated into these tools allows for the provision of real-time feedback on reading patterns, which assists users in recognizing and modifying behaviors that are inefficient. Furthermore, several programs make use of algorithms to modify the presentation of text, thereby presenting it in a manner that maximizes both the speed of reading and the comprehension of the material. For instance, approaches such as Rapid Serial Visual Presentation (RSVP) offer words or phrases in rapid succession at the center of the screen. This reduces the amount of eye movement that occurs and increases the pace at which one can read on the screen.

Maintaining a diverse approach is required in order to keep up with the latest research and approaches in the field of speed reading. At the outset, it is of the utmost importance to become familiar with the academic literature and research studies that have been published in journals that are associated with cognitive psychology, education, and neuroscience. A deeper understanding of the most recent discoveries and developments in the subject can be gained from these sources. When it comes to gaining access to research papers and publications that have been reviewed by peers, online databases such as PubMed, Google Scholar, and JSTOR are extremely helpful resources. Additionally, attending academic conferences and seminars on reading and literacy can provide an opportunity to learn from professionals in the field as well as network with scholars and practitioners in the field.

Monitoring the activities of thought leaders and organizations that are committed to literacy and speed reading is yet another efficient method for staying up to date. With the use of blogs, social media, and newsletters, a great number of academics, educators, and authors share their discoveries and views with the world. When you subscribe to these platforms, you will receive regular updates on new methods, findings from research, and helpful advice for boosting your reading speed and comprehension. In addition, becoming a member of a professional organization such as the Association for Psychological Science (APS) or the International Literacy Association (ILA) can grant access to a variety of unique resources, publications, and events.

Staying up to date with the latest strategies for speed reading can also be accomplished by participating in online training programs and various courses. Numerous educational institutions and online platforms provide classes that teach students not just the fundamentals of speed reading but also more sophisticated tactics and the most recent findings from research. In order to improve the quality of the learning experience, these classes frequently incorporate interactive components such as quizzes, exercises, and conversations with classmates. In addition, there are programs that give certification, which can be a very useful credential for professionals, trainers, and educators who are looking to demonstrate their proficiency in speed reading.

For the purpose of preserving and enhancing one's skills, it is essential to engage in consistent practice of speed reading and to implement new strategies. In order to strengthen new habits and make them feel like second nature, constant practice is required, just as it is with any other skill. It is possible to integrate new approaches better and monitor progress by setting aside a specific amount of time each day for the purpose of practicing speed reading. When it comes to improving versatility and adaptation in speed reading, using a variety of reading materials, ranging from fictional novels to academic articles, can be of great assistance. In addition, maintaining a reading notebook in which one records strategies, observations, and areas in which one could better contribute to the development of significant insights and motivation.

In addition to this, it is essential to conduct an in-depth analysis of the efficiency of newly developed methods and instruments. As a result of individual variances in cognitive capacities, learning styles, and reading goals, not all strategies are equally effective for everyone. Instead, the outcomes can vary depending on the individual. It is possible to evaluate which strategies are the most effective by conducting self-evaluations and soliciting input from those who are considered to be peers or mentors. In addition, maintaining an awareness of the potential limitations and downsides of particular approaches can help the prevention of the implementation of techniques that are either unproductive or harmful.

If you are interested in fast reading, working together with other people who have the same interest can be beneficial. A supportive environment that allows for the sharing of experiences, the discussion of new techniques, and the exchange of feedback can be provided by activities such as study groups, book clubs, or online forums. Learning through collaboration can result in the discovery of a variety of tactics and points of view, which can expand one's understanding of speed-reading methods and provide opportunities for their implementation. Furthermore, teaching others about speed reading can help one strengthen their own knowledge and abilities, as it is sometimes necessary to have a profound comprehension of the subject matter in order to explain concepts and strategies involved in speed reading.

In conclusion, it is necessary to maintain a healthy lifestyle in order to maximize cognitive abilities connected to reading and comprehension. Getting enough sleep, engaging in regular physical activity, and maintaining a healthy diet are all factors that contribute to general brain health and have the potential to improve focus, memory, and processing speed. Practicing mindfulness, which includes activities like meditation and deep breathing exercises, can also help enhance focus and reduce stress, thus generating an environment that is conducive to reading effectively. Understanding the interrelationship between one's physical and mental health and one's cognitive function highlights the need to take a holistic approach to maintaining one's proficiency in speed reading and remaining up to date with the latest information.

In conclusion, maintaining current knowledge of the latest techniques and research in the field of speed reading is a dynamic and continuing process that necessitates engagement with academic literature, technology, professional networks, and consistent practice. The continual improvements in this discipline are highlighted by the development of techniques for rapid reading, which are informed by cognitive psychology and neuroscience. It is possible to improve one's speed reading abilities by embracing new approaches and tools, conducting an in-depth analysis of how effective they are, and working in conjunction with other people. In addition, leading a healthy lifestyle helps to boost cognitive functions that are necessary for effective reading and comprehension. Those who are interested in navigating and succeeding in our information-rich world should make it a priority to keep themselves abreast of the most recent advancements in speed reading. This is because the terrain of information is constantly expanding.

CONCLUSION

To sum up, "Speed Reading: Accelerate Your Learning and Comprehension: Techniques and Strategies to Read Faster and Retain More" gives you the necessary tools to change the way you read completely. You will improve your comprehension and information retention while also increasing your reading speed by implementing the methods and strategies covered in this book. You will be able to read anything more effectively and efficiently thanks to this dual concentration.

Throughout the book, there is a thorough framework for honing your speed-reading skills through hands-on activities and real-world applications. The book's emphasis on promoting visual processing and kicking bad habits like subvocalization emphasizes its dedication to comprehensive and long-lasting improvement. Furthermore, you may modify your speed-reading techniques to fit any situation, whether it be personal, professional, or academic, thanks to strategies designed specifically for different kinds of books.

"Speed Reading" is an approachable manual for readers of all skill levels since it tackles typical problems and offers ways to solve them. By the time you finish the book, you'll have completely changed the way you read, giving you the ability to handle information overload better and keep up with our fast-paced society.

In the end, "Speed Reading: Accelerate Your Learning and Comprehension" is a doorway to a more knowledgeable and capable version of yourself, not merely a manual. Accept the methods herein, and watch as your reading proficiency soars, opening up fresh avenues for development.

Thank you for buying and reading/ listening to our book. If you found this book useful/ helpful please take a few minutes and leave a review on the platform where you purchased our book. Your feedback matters greatly to us.